Ethical
PORN
for
DICKS

A MAN'S GUIDE TO
RESPONSIBLE VIEWING
PLEASURE

David J. Ley, Ph.D.
Sexual Health Alliance Edition

First Published in 2016 by
ThreeL Media | Stone Bridge Press
P. O. Box 8208, Berkeley, CA 94707
www.threelmedia.com

Sexual Health Alliance Edition
Reprinted on May 2021
www.sexualhealthalliance.com

Printed in the United States of America.

Contents

Foreword

Notes from a Feminist Pornographer

Tristan Taormino

I'm really glad you found this book. Why? Because there is so much hand-wringing, shame, guilt, pain, and panic surrounding porn in our culture. Anti-porn crusaders on the left and the right want to convince us that all of society's ills would be cured if we just stopped watching so much porn. Porn has always been a convenient target and scapegoat for our collective freak-outs about sexual desire, power, and freedom. Young people don't have a clue about the realities of sex? Blame porn. Sexually transmitted infections on the rise? Blame porn. Couples have communication troubles, performance anxiety, and so-called "sexual dysfunction" in the bedroom? Blame porn. Monogamous marriage deeply unsatisfying for many people? Blame porn.

We desperately need an antidote to the morality police and the junk science behind these panics, and that antidote is *Ethical Porn for Dicks*. Dr. David Ley cuts through all the bullshit and writes candidly about a topic that, for all its raw nakedness on screen, gets overdressed in lots of fancy adornments in the name of public health and decency. He brings an important conversation out of the closet—even out of the privacy of a therapist's office—and into the light of day. He demystifies all the hype about how porn is rewiring our brains and destroying the fabric of society. And, very importantly, he reveals the extreme bias and

9

very shaky "research" behind some of the most popular declarations and statistics we hear about porn again and again. He challenges said research and exposes it for what it really is: the moral policing of pleasure. In this book, he breaks down false binaries with gems of wisdom. He is so straightforward, so unabashed and unapologetic that your brain *will* feel re-wired after reading this book—in a good way.

When people feel ashamed, lost, conflicted, or confused when it comes to sex, they look for simple explanations—and there's porn with its cheesy lighting and predictable plotlines, ready to stand in for what's really bothering us. We've all read the headlines: porn ruins marriage, porn is coming between you and your partner (ironic, right?). What's actually happening is this: we have internalized puritanical and negative ideas about sex, we have no models for honest sexual communication, and we rarely see diverse depictions of sexuality in any media. As a result, we've all got hang-ups, misinformation, and insecurities, and we are afraid to admit we have them or look at why we do. So when someone else demonizes porn, we can latch on and say, "yeah, there's the culprit." Then we don't have to look at our unrealistic expectations about love and sex, our isolation and fear, our untreated mental health issues, and our outdated relationship models.

In fact, we have lost the ability to look at this medium called pornography as just that: *a medium*, one kind of pop culture consumed by the masses with highs and lows that reflect the culture in which it is created and imagine possibilities beyond it. Instead of looking at porn alongside television, Hollywood films, music, video games, the Web, magazines, and other media, we relegate it to its own dingy corner on the wrong side of the railroad tracks. We project our insecurities and fears onto it, making it into a face-fucking boogeyman. But the truth is that porn is not one monolithic thing. Just as no one says, "All television is bad," or, "All movies are good," we cannot look at porn and make a blanket judgment about it. Porn comes from multi-million-dollar corporations and from independent producers. It's part of the big capitalist machine and it's on the fringes of the art world. It's luxurious, cheap, tacky, stylish, wild, weird, boring, sloppy, enlightening, groundbreaking, stupid, smart, offensive, repetitive, experimental, one-dimensional, sexist, feminist, political, realistic, unbelievable, racist, anti-racist, sexy, off-putting, universal, niche, celebratory, scary, amusing, serious, fantastical, educational, mind-numbing, thought-provoking, stimulating, off-putting, and any combination of these descriptors. The point is this: porn is complex, and our attitudes should reflect—not reduce—that complexity.

Our sexual culture and ideas are always changing. Sexual norms and taboos have continually evolved as time has marched on. Until the early 20th century, women could only get a vibrator—which replaced time-consuming manual treatment (hand jobs)—from a doctor after they were diagnosed with hysteria or frigidity. Gay people were considered mentally ill by psychologists before homosexuality was completely removed as a disorder from the Diagnostic and Statistical Manual of Mental Disorders (DSM) in 1987. Going down on your partner was illegal in many places in the US until the Supreme Court ruled on *Lawrence v. Texas* in 2003. Lots of sex acts we think of as normal and ordinary—including oral sex—were deemed racy and unconventional (and even illegal) at one point in time. So while change itself is nothing new, the advent of the Internet and new technologies have sped up the process. One clear example is the dramatic shift in the production costs, distribution, accessibility, and diversity of pornography. Never before has there been more porn or pornmakers.

Nowadays, seemingly everyone has their hand in the porn pie. The Kardashian empire we know today was launched by the widespread popularity of then-little-known Kim Kardashian's sex tape. Celebrities returned to the spotlight with their own home movies (Oh hi, Tommy Lee and Pamela Anderson). Steven Soderbergh made *The Girlfriend Experience*, proving that even acclaimed filmmakers could get in on the game. Why has porn proven to be a successful vehicle to get people talking and increase visibility? Because it's a medium that reaches a ton of people from all walks of life. It crosses lines of gender, race, class, sexual orientation, geography, ability, and religion. Because we cannot get enough of it.

Speaking of enough, the amount of porn we watch has been positioned as a measure of our characters. While anti-porn movements have been around for decades, a relatively recent phenomenon is how porn *consumption* has been easily conflated with *addiction* models by a growing part of the psychological/therapeutic industry. This new problem of "porn addiction," which is often linked to "sex addiction," is a way for society to further police our sexuality. Equating porn with addiction has proven to be very easily marketable. Sex and porn addiction serve as both a shorthand people can understand ("He's an addict! He needs help!") and a get-out-of-jail-free card, especially for public figures ("Majority celebrity headed to rehab for porn addiction"). It's also proven to be very profitable: sex and porn addiction specialists found a way to capitalize on people's anxieties about sexuality and make tons of money off it. There are no solid statistics on exactly how much money is generated by sex and porn addiction treatment, but it's part of an overall addiction rehab industry that raked in $35 billion in 2014 alone.

This new trend to pathologize and monetize people's consumption of sexual material is further proof that we need more diverse perspectives in public discussions about porn, and more voices like David Ley's to remind people what we should already know. As Ley writes in these pages, "It's possible to be an ethical, responsible person and treat oneself and others with dignity and integrity, AND to watch hot, no-holds-barred sex on screen."

As a feminist pornographer dedicated to making ethical porn, I want you to ethically consume porn by paying for it and feeling turned on, amazed, curious, and free when you watch it. I do not make porn for people to view and feel bad about themselves. I do not wake up each morning and think, "How can I make something that will prey on people's worst fears?" or, "I really hope my porn gets in the way of intimacy between partners," or, "How can I reduce someone to their body parts and strip them of their humanity and their agency?" It's quite the opposite. I make porn to show you what should not be mystified, hidden, or secret. I make porn so that you can see yourself represented on screen or see someone completely different from you. I make porn so that you can have a language to describe your desires, fantasies, wants, and needs. I make porn so we can all see how (and how long it really takes) to warm up for anal sex! I make porn to give people the sex education they never got elsewhere. I make porn to help people live out their fantasies. I make porn to be a tool for your arousal, your pleasure, your stress relief, your orgasms. I know that people use my porn in different ways for diverse reasons, and I can appreciate all the how's and why's of your porn viewing. I am not interested in measuring your porn use against some made-up norm or deciding if you're using porn properly or not. Watch it, pause it, fast-forward it, re-watch it however you want—just buy it (so we can keep making more).

David Ley and this book are voices of reason among all the porn panic. As he unpacks the moral judgments, fallacy, and hypocrisy about pornography in our culture, he reveals truths that go way beyond porn. He dares to dive into the murky pool of our desires, our fears, and all the fucked-up ways we approach sex in society. In that way, porn is revealed as a piece of the puzzle, one that is both the catch-all for everything we want *and* one that's been elevated beyond its actual place in our lives. This book is an invaluable tool to help us stop demonizing porn. Instead, we need to look to it as a beacon of information we can use to understand more about our sexual desires, dreams, fears, and triggers; a key to our sexual pasts and futures; or, if you prefer, something to get you off.

Introduction

What This Book Is and Isn't

I wrote this book imagining that I'm sitting and having a beer or two, talking with friends about porn. I might mention research and highbrow concepts, but I'm not going to bog you down with references, citations, or footnotes.

I'm not going to talk to you like you're a patient I'm treating. I'm not going to talk you like you're a reporter, or a scholar or a scientist. I'm writing this as though you're a buddy of mine who is asking me questions they've been concerned about, afraid to ask, and unable to answer. Why would men be unwilling to ask these questions? Because they're afraid of being judged, called a pervert, a porn addict, treated as though they are a potential rapist, or simply seen as scuzzy because they're admitting they watch porn. They can't confess that they look at dirty magazines, specifically for the pictures, screw the boring articles about hi-fi stereos.

There's a resource list at the end of the book, and if you are desperate to understand more of the science behind this stuff, or the origins of my comments, you can check out those materials.

Here's a warning—I cuss. Sorry. I figure, if you're interested in reading and thinking about your use of porn, seeing me write the words fuck, dick, screw, etc., isn't going to make your head explode. If it does, well, I'm really fucking sorry for you that you can't handle dirty words. I just read some research that people

15

who cuss more tend to be more honest, open and confident. I'm not bullshitting you, or hiding morality behind bad research. In fact, every time you read a cussword in here—just think, "Wow, David is being really fucking honest with me right now." When I don't know something in here—I'll tell you.

There's a reason I'm writing about this, in this way. A bunch of reasons in fact.

- I'm told that guys don't buy a lot of books these days. Publisher after publisher told me that if I wanted to write this book, I had to write it for women, for female readers. But guys are the ones with the concerns, the unanswered questions. Guys are the ones watching the porn and then being thrown under the bus for it.
- I could quote lots of research and citations at you, and you could disagree and throw other citations at me. Unless we were all drunk and started throwing wadded up research papers at each other, this doesn't sound fun.
- The sad fact is that most of the science about porn is really crappy. In fact, an overwhelming majority of everything written about porn is pretty crappy. Because the people writing it, whether it is research, books, or news articles, start with a certain opinion in mind about porn, and they write and research in order to support that conclusion.

You have certain opinions about porn. And so do I. Just like climate change, vaccines and politics, the more science and evidence I throw at you in support of my opinion—the stronger your opposition to my opinion gets. The only thing such evidence does is solidify your opinions on one side or the other.

- There are tons of things written about porn, describing how dangerous and damaging it is to men, women, and society.
- There are also many (though relatively fewer) things written about how wonderful porn is and why you should "learn to fuck like a porn star."
- This book is neither one of those.

I'm not out to scare you about porn, even though there are some scary issues I will discuss. I'm also not going to glorify or idealize porn. I know a bunch of porn stars now. Some I like, some I don't. Some porn disturbs me, and some I think is hot.

I view porn the same as any other human activity or endeavor. Like television, space travel, and politics, there are good things about porn and there are bad things. This book is intended to offer you the ability to make responsible decisions about porn, knowing both sides. Unlike most of the people out there writing about porn, I believe you have the intelligence, self-control and maturity to make your own decisions. In that, I think this book is unique. I talk a lot in this book about differences between men and women. These differences may not apply to you—they mean little at the individual level. But they can help us understand larger issues, and how to change things.

About the Illustrations

Just about a mile from my home in Albuquerque, New Mexico, lies a sprawling piece of desert and volcanic rock cliffs, designated as the Petroglyph National Monument. Filled with rock carvings, the area was a favorite canvas for artists and shamans throughout the past millennia. Many of the drawings, chiseled painstakingly into the stone, are unashamedly sexual.

At left is one of my favorites, a fellow I call simply "Penis Man." This guy is proud of his big cock.

Opposite is how the image appears today. Catholic settlers in the area, as far back as the 1600s, found this fellow's naked penis to be offensive, a pagan and pornographic image. The cross below him was likely carved into the stone in an effort to counteract the pagan power of his pornographic penis.

In other areas of the Southwest, this earliest form of erotic art was defaced or chiseled away, lest people be corrupted by these images. Images depicting fertility rites, sexual instruction, and just plain celebrating sex were destroyed. Many of the drawings from the Southwest depict Kokopelli, a trickster fertility figure, who was typically depicted with a flute and an erection. But today, most commercial images of Kokopelli have been sanitized, because the modern world can't handle his penis. In the Australian outback, rock art that shows orgies, genitalia, and fabulous sex is hidden away. Some sites traditionally only allowed adult men to view them, lest people be corrupted by these ancient images of lust.

I've illustrated this book with drawings of what I call "Petro-porn." As far back as man has had intelligence, he—and she—has loved sex and has recorded images that show how much eroticism means to us. Thousands of years before the Polaroid, people were chipping away at rock walls to create lasting images of the amazing sex they'd had the night before, even if that sex were only in their imagination.

Petro-porn is found in every region of the world—China, Siberia, the American Southwest, Alaska, Algeria, the Alps, the Australian Outback, African wilds, and in South American pyramids. Group sex, masturbation, bestiality, and homosexuality is found in these images. Dicks are huge and hard, breasts and buttocks are round and firm. Women are usually shown lying back, legs spread, and ready

for sex. The people in these images are shown enjoying them-selves with smiles and orgasms. There are money shots where men are ejaculating, and there are women directing other men and women as they copulate gleefully with men, donkeys, and jackals.

The lost, and rediscovered, paintings of Pompeii depict orgies, passionate sex, orgasms, and erotic passion. So do the beautiful sculptures that adorn temples in Khajuraho, India, demonstrating the Hindu traditions of the Kama Sutra.

Today's obsession with Internet porn is only the latest, most modern chapter in this tale. I defy anyone to find images in modern porn on the Internet, which don't have ancient ances-tors in drawings, sculpture, and rock carvings, whether hundreds of years or millennia old. Sadly, the modern fear of pornography also has long roots. The people today who want to ban or re-strict Internet porn have ancestors who chipped away at rock images of sex or chiseled in crosses to counteract the power of a penis.

I've chosen to illustrate this book with these images, ac-knowledging the long, rich history of artistic depictions of the erotic. I use these images with respect, admiration, and deep re-gard for our ancestors and what these images meant to them. I've drawn these images from petroglyphs I've found myself, from those shared with me by friends, and from images in works such as the delightful book *The Serpent and the Sacred Fire* by Dennis Slifer. I've occasionally taken some artistic license of my own with the images.

By the way—if you watch these images on cave walls, to the light of a campfire, the images flicker in delightfully por-nographic stop-motion ways. Our ancestors were some smart, horny bastards. Gotta love them.

How to Read This Book

Read this book any damn way you want. Read it cover to cover in one sitting if you want. Read it one part at a time, sitting on the toilet. Flip around the book, reading sections at random. The book is organized in general sections around some of the basic issues that come up around porn, in men's lives. Hopefully that makes it easier for you to find the things you're most interested in.

Acknowledgments

No book is written alone. I've learned that through the tremendous support and kindness of so many people. Thanks to Gregory Kaplan and Tina Horn of ThreeL Media for believing in me and this project. Thanks to Jiz Lee for helping me come up with the brilliant title. Thanks to first readers David Hersh, Tony Dipasquale, Adam Safron, Heather McPherson, Dylan Davies, Michael Whiteacre, Craig Perra, and others. Thanks to so many in the adult industry who were willing to share their experiences, thoughts, and time with me to help me understand their work, their needs, and their concerns. Dr. Kelsey Obsession, Mercedes Carrera, Shine Louise Houston, Lucie Bee, Conner Habib, and Brett Hall at Pornhub were all so helpful. Special thanks to the folks at Kink.com for their support, and for Eric Paul Leue's kind assistance. Kim Wallen—thanks for the support and guidance on the "petro-porn." There are so many in the sexuality education and therapy world who have helped and supported this project. Hernando Chavez, Nikky Prause, Jim Pfaus, Paul Joannides, Michael Aaron, Mike Bailey, Dan Savage, Marty Klein, Joe Kort, Robert King, Jess O'Reilly, Kate Frank, Justin Lehmiller, Barry Reay, Rebecca Sullivan, Alan McKee, Jay Blevins, Megan Andelloux, Shira Tarrant, Neil Malamuth, Laci Green, Meredith Chavez, Richard Sprott, David Ortmann, Michael

Seto, Ken Zucker, Roger Libby, Chris Donaghue, Buster Ross and so many, many more. I truly am blessed to stand on the shoulders of so many great people. Sorry about the spiked heels. When I started this work and advocacy, I felt very alone. Now, I have more friends and supporters than I ever believed possible. I'm deeply honored.

True thanks to the folks at Southwest Sexual Health Alliance, and at Cross County Education, who supported my work and passion for educating therapists about sex. Thanks to the kind and helpful folks at the FBI Cyber Crimes Unit for taking the time to answer my questions, and a special thanks for not arresting me for asking them! Thanks to Lawrence Walters and Myles Jackman for taking time to answer my legal questions.

Thanks to Katie Couric, who just wants to hear about common sense and enough of that research crap—this book's for you.

Special acknowledgment and shout-outs to Chanel Preston and Tristan Taormino for their inspiring, insightful, and educational contributions.

Watching Porn While Having, Not Being, a Dick

You Are NOT a Dick Just Because You Watch Porn

I wrote this book for all the people out there who feel shame and guilt over their porn use. In my mind, guilt is when you feel bad about something you did. Shame is when you feel bad about who and what you are. Shame is when you are told that your poor choices reflect something unchangeable about who and what you are. Many people feel guilty about watching porn and feel like it's a dirty secret. Sometimes, that little bit of seedy dirtiness is actually part of the turn on.

But many more people are told today that watching porn makes them a bad person, and it's something they should be ashamed of. We are told that watching porn is bad for society, women, and women's role in society. It warps kids' brains and is destroying all that is beautiful about sex and love. Basically, we are told that every time we watch porn, a baby seal gets strangled to death with XXX-rated videotape. That a real man wouldn't need or want to watch porn because he can get all the "real sex" he wants or needs and because masturbation to porn is for weaklings. That a "good man" wouldn't be able to get turned on by watching porn, knowing it might have been made by exploiting women.

It's hard not to take that in and start to view yourself as a dick because you watch porn. To start to worry that you are weak, unethical, and a pervert because you watch porn. But I believe it is possible to be a gentleman and watch porn. It's possible to be an ethical, responsible person and treat oneself and others with dignity and integrity, AND to watch hot, no-holds-barred sex on screen.

This book is intended to give you a framework to make your own decision, your own assessment, and your own plan about how you want to ethically, mindfully, and consciously incorporate pornography into your life. I believe the first step is in dealing with your shame over porn use. Let's start there.

Belief in Porn Addiction Is Really about Shame

If you watch porn these days and worry about it, it's hard not to end up worried that you're a porn addict. That label is thrown around on the Internet, on television, and by wives and girlfriends.

Believing that you are a porn addict actually makes things worse. Research has found that people who believe they are porn addicts experience more distress, more worry, more fear, and more pain than other people, regardless of how much porn they actually watch. The label of porn addict has become a form of shame and fear towards our desires for sex, masturbation, and visual stimulation.

So, if you are adopting the label of porn addict, you are telling yourself that there is something wrong with you. And you're telling yourself that porn is more powerful than you are.

Right now, you're a person who is feeling ashamed and scared of your porn use. But you're reading this book. I hope that reading it helps you understand what porn is for you, demystifies it, and makes you less afraid of it. Ultimately, that's my goal and the point of this book.

Yes, I Watch Porn

Like a lot of guys, I remember the first porn I ever saw. A friend down the street gave me a picture cut out of a magazine,

Penthouse I think, and I took it home and looked it for hours. I can't remember if I masturbated. I'm pretty sure I did, but funnily enough, that experience in my memory is less about that orgasm and more about the mental experience of seeing the sexuality of another person.

My interest was less about my sexual stimulation, and much, much more about a fascination with the idea that another person, a woman, could be sexually confident enough to pose nude for the sexual enjoyment of other people. I've always found such sexual confidence incredibly appealing. I still remember that the picture was of a bombshell brunette. I don't know if I liked curvy, dark-haired women before then, but I've loved them ever since.

I'm exposed to a lot of different kinds of porn and material through my work and practice. Some I find extremely arousing and titillating. Others I find interesting, but they might not really do it for me. I've watched porn with groups of therapists and students, as a part of classes I teach. Sometimes, those porn videos were ones I specifically chose because I found them arousing. Other times they were diverse depictions that I chose in order to show the students the great range of material that's out there. There's porn that I'm not interested in seeing, though I recognize other people can watch it and still be healthy. I don't like most reality television, but I don't think other people are sick for liking it.

Watching sex videos with classes, I didn't find myself struggling to hide a boner. So, just because I might like a certain kind of porn doesn't mean it has an irresistible hold over me. I think the same is true for most people. I pursue different kinds of porn at different times for different reasons. When I've watched porn with partners, I've often watched different porn than when I watch it by myself. If I'm stressed out, I sometimes choose one flavor of porn, and when I just had an exciting experience or fantasy, I might try to find a porn that mimics that situation.

I have patients and friends who are incredibly rigid about their favorite kind of porn, and others who will watch almost anything. I tend to be in between those poles. I have many colleagues who suggest that people use porn to increase libido and to "jump-start" sexual arousal. For those people, porn can be a medicine, prescribed to overcome the many things in daily life that conspire to suppress sexual arousal.

This book is written from the experience of a psychologist, a therapist, and a scientist, who has studied, treated, written about and spoken/debated about porn use. But it's also written from the experience of a man, who, like most, has had porn as a part of my sexuality throughout most of my life. My goal is to try to integrate those views.

What Is Porn Anyway?

Historically, "pornography" is a Greek term that described things that were written about prostitutes. Today, the term is incredibly broad and often used in a negative manner. Some people work really hard to distinguish pornography from erotica. Unfortunately, those distinctions are often in the eye of the beholder. Some people call *Fifty Shades of Grey* porn; others call it erotica. The distinction seems to be whether the person approves of the material.

Today, the word porn has been used to describe lots of random things. There's "science porn," "space porn," and "mommy porn." There's "porn for women," which is mostly pictures and videos of men doing housework. In none of these things is there any sex involved and certainly no sex workers.

Even in the world of sexual material called pornography,

there's lots of variance. There are still images that are "soft" like *Playboy Magazine*, and still images that are "hardcore" like *HUSTLER*. There are videos that are soft and videos that are hardcore. There are videos that have a plot and hardcore sex, and videos that are just hardcore sex.

There's written material, ranging from the graphic written descriptions of sex in romance novels to *Penthouse Letters* and the website Literotica.

There's amateur material, commercial and professionally produced videos and images, and stuff that lies in between, like professionally made porn involving amateurs.

Internet pornography includes videos you can watch online AND includes amateurs and professionals that you can have video chats with. The Naked Therapist, Sarah White, does online therapy sessions where she gets naked in front of the camera. Is that porn? Maybe, maybe not.

The wide, wide (gaping?) world of porn is one where the boundaries keep growing, every day, as technology changes. People's reactions to these different types of porn vary between people and between different times. A few years ago, people were very worried about phone sexlines. Those are still out there, though we hear less about them, as many people who used to use such lines are now turning to other forms of sexual entertainment available online and other places. Every few years, we hear that the porn of today is far more graphic and destructive than porn of yesteryear. That could be true, but when I look back at vintage porn, or petro-porn, I see much of what exists today.

Porn is many different things. Much of what is written about porn relies on general, simplistic descriptions of what porn is, by people who don't actually understand the great diversity of what porn includes. And, these are usually people who want to tell you that the porn you are using is unhealthy. I DO understand that porn includes lots of material that is diverse and is constantly changing as technology changes. But, I can't tailor this book and discussion to address every tiny niche and type of porn. The book would NEVER be finished—because porn is changing every day.

The specific type of porn you use might or might not be discussed in this book. But, if you're concerned about it—its impact on you or your life—you can probably glean some ideas from the information we discuss.

I'm just going to use the blanket term porn to describe lots of things involving lots of sexually explicit material. Why? Because that's how guys are using the term. I don't think porn is a negative word. I think it's a neutral term, which we get to define and claim however we would like.

Porn Can Be Ethical

I like to talk about my writing with people in my life. Not just friends and family, but strangers and acquaintances. It gives me an insight into how people respond outside the "echo chamber effect." The best, most honest response came from an older female family friend, who asked me bluntly, "CAN porn be ethical?"

Now, I'm not saying here that porn is moral—morality is about whether something is right or wrong, and most things connected to sex when it's not about love or making babies are just assumed to be immoral. Moral views of sex are often based on conservative, usually religiously based, values. Maybe "moral porn" is the next battlefield. I'm not sure what moral porn might look like, but I'm interested to see.

But ethics are about doing things the right way. It's not just about following the laws, but about being mindful, conscious, and deliberate about what you do, with the intent of having integrity. An old story asks you to consider what you would do if you were hiding Jews in your basement in the 1940s in Germany and the Nazis knocked at your door. Telling the truth might actually be immoral, as it would result in those people's deaths in concentration camps. But lying to save them is actually unethical, as we hold up the principle that truth-telling is critical and important. (To be clear, in that circumstance, I'd lie like a sonuvabitch).

In most situations, following the rules of ethics and the laws are the way we aspire to morality. There are problems when the laws of a society support immorality (such as during segregation, the days of slavery, or when homosexuality was illegal in the United States—note that it still is in many countries around the world). Today, in the United States, our laws protect free speech, sexual freedom, self-determination, and against discrimination. Our laws also prohibit rape and illegal exploitation and require sexual consent. These ethics, these rules, are upholding the moral values of free will, protection from harm, and fairness. Can pornography be ethical within those rules?

Two professors, Australian professor Alan McKee and Canadian researcher Rebecca Sullivan, wrote a book called *Pornography: Structures, Agency and Performance* that reviews all the research to date about pornography. In it, they say something very powerful:

> Our claim isn't that pornography is "good," but that we must strive to make it better.

Porn star and sexologist Annie Sprinkle has said something similar:

> The answer to bad porn isn't no porn . . . it's to try and make better porn.

In a nutshell, these statements sum up ethical porn. Ethical porn is about recognizing that porn is vulnerable to being harmful, exploitive, and misused. But the answer isn't to throw it out with the bathwater.

Porn, for better or worse, is here to stay. In the US, it is protected under free speech, and it needs to be because if we lose the right of free sexual expression, we lose many other critical protections. Porn, as illustrated by the cave drawings in this book, has been around as long as humanity. Attempts to get rid of porn are just more likely to drive it underground, where it is secret and hidden. And under such secrecy, people are more likely to get hurt or taken advantage of, and lose the ability to freely consent. When organized crime is involved in making and distributing porn, as it was fifty years ago (and is not any longer) just how likely is it, do you think, that a performer can assert his/her boundaries and have them respected?

But porn can be better than it is. And the principles of ethical porn strive to get it there. Ethical porn is not just about who makes the porn or how it's made. It's also about how it's used. That's where you come in. When you watch porn, you are voting, as it were, for that type of porn, that style of porn, and for the people who made it.

We, the people who watch porn, can and should start to "vote" with our mouses, our smartphones, our computers, our fingers, our eyes, and yes, even with our dicks. We can vote supporting porn that is:

- Made legally
- Respects the rights of performers
- Pays performers for their labor
- Respects the copyright of the producer
- Shows both fantasy sex AND real-world sex, so that we can see and explore both
- Is as diverse as the people consuming it—showing all the thirty-one million different flavors of people that are out there
- Celebrates sexuality as a diverse, complex and multi-faceted component of being human, without saying there is a right or wrong way to be sexual
- Is made by people who are trying to make "better porn"
- And is watched by people who want there to BE "better porn"
- Treats both performers and consumers of porn as free, consenting, thinking and powerful beings

Ethical porn is, in my mind, more of an action than a category. When we think of ethical porn as something we do, as opposed to something that simply is, we recognize it is about "striving." This way, it is always something we can keep doing, and doing better. And this way, when a maker of ethical porn makes a mistake or is shown to have produced or distributed something that wasn't what they thought it was, we don't simply say, "See, porn is bad, even when it tries to be ethical." Instead, we say, "See, it can be hard to make ethical porn and that's why we have to keep trying."

It's not just about the porn maker. It's about you. The makers of ethical porn won't survive, the principles of ethical porn won't endure, if YOU don't support them. Porn makers exist in symbiosis, in connection, with the people who watch it.

Ethical porn is a partnership. A sexy, slippery, hot, heavy, and dirty partnership between people who love to fuck in front of cameras and people who love to watch them do it.

Porn Use Is a Silly Thing to Keep Secret (But We Do)

We keep our porn use secret because of shame. It's as simple as that. Today, there's a raging moral war on sex, and pornography is the front line of the battle.

"Don't ask, don't tell" describes any number of different sexual issues, including porn use. If a person's connection to porn becomes a public issue, they're doomed. This happens when a person like a teacher is exposed as having done porn

or even sent their husband a sexy picture, or when a person gets caught watching porn at work. When a person's connection to porn becomes public, outside their home or their friends, they're in deep shit, drowning in moral condemnation. Everyone turns away and pretends they don't even know what porn is, much less know that person.

The easy availability of porn through the Internet

is turning many things on its head. Most especially, the many different rules that society has used to control people's sexuality are being undermined and weakened.

Before Internet porn, people with various kinky fetishes thought they were alone and that everyone else was normal but them. Gays, lesbians and bisexuals likewise thought they were abnormal and had to keep their desires secret, as they suffered in solitary sexual silence.

Throughout history, societies have maintained power by enforcing conformity, limiting expression, and suppressing groups who might challenge the illusion that there is any one, right way to be—or be sexual.

Before the days of effective contraception and disease prevention, societies HAD to enforce controls on sexual behavior. Otherwise, there would be babies that couldn't be supported. Before women achieved their well-earned level of economic equality (at least, approaching economic equality, it's not there yet), they HAD to treat sexual gratification as a scarce, begrudgingly offered resource or face loss of the one resource they controlled.

Society is changing, though, and dramatically. I'm not making too much of the Internet and the porn that is there. Look, it's just porn after all. Right?

But, think about it. Now that lonely, geeky guy, ignored by all the girls in his grade (we're talking about me at age thirteen, just to be clear), can go home and look at videos of beautiful women having sex and imagine himself with them. He can masturbate, take the edge off, and not feel so lonely and excluded.

Consider this. Throughout human history, societies that allowed polygamy (one man with multiple wives/concubines) had higher levels of violent crime. Why? Because in those societies, the wealthy, powerful men took all the hot women. And the streets were filled with young, bored men with nothing to lose.

One argument for monogamous societies is that they have lower crime because those men are now trying to put food on their tables for their wives and kids, rather than being out there kicking up trouble. Throughout human history, access to sexual material—whether it's pornography, education or contraception—has been limited to the powerful and wealthy. Many of the caches of petro-porn in Australia, Pompeii, and other places were restricted to view by men and the wealthy elite. For one reason or another, societies have worked to keep sexual knowledge and freedom from being generally accessible to the "common man," as well as from women, the poor, and the disenfranchised. Feminists call this "sexual privilege."

The easy, free access to porn on the Internet undermines these social dynamics, which have been affecting behaviors and relationships for thousands of years. What if suddenly, people (men and women) don't HAVE to choose to keep their sexual desires secret, to accept relationships merely because they feel they are supposed to, are able to reach a reasonable level of sexual satisfaction without giving up their privacy and autonomy? We have no idea. I think it's fascinating. Porn on the Internet is a remarkable tool of democracy in very interesting ways. Nowadays, societies with greater access to porn have lower rates of sex crimes. Porn on the Internet is a part of making the world a better place, where we lie less about sex, and get to stop pretending there is one right way to have sex.

Porn Is Not the Problem—YOU Are

Porn is not addictive. Sex is not addictive. The ideas of porn and sex addiction are pop psychology concepts that seem to make sense but have no legitimate scientific basis. For decades, these concepts have flourished in pop culture but have been repeatedly rejected by medicine and mental health. The media has accepted that sex and porn are addictive because it seems intuitively true—we all feel sometimes that we might do something stupid or self-destructive when turned on.

But this false belief is dangerous and ultimately not helpful. Because when people buy into the belief that porn is addictive, it changes the argument. All of a sudden, it seems like porn and sex are the problems. Porn addiction becomes a label, and seems to be an explanation, when in fact, it is just meaningless words that distract from the real issue. But sex and porn aren't the problems. You are.

People have a strong response to video pornography. The economic forces of the open market have driven modern Internet porn to be very effective at triggering male sexual buttons.

But women actually have a stronger physiological response to porn than men, and based upon this research, women should be more addicted to pornography than men. But the overwhelming majority of the stories we hear about are men. Why is this? Because one part of this issue is an attack on aspects of male sexuality, including masturbation and the use of pornography—behaviors that society fears and wants to suppress.

Porn can affect people (by turning them on), but it does not take them over or override their values. If someone watches porn showing something they find distasteful, it has no impact on their behavior or desires. But, if someone watches porn showing acts that they, the watcher, are positive or at least neutral about, it does make them slightly more likely to express interest in trying that act themselves.

Take anal sex for instance. If a porn viewer finds it disgusting, watching anal pornography isn't going to change that. But, if they are positive or neutral on the idea of buttsex, then watching anal porn will slightly increase the chance that they would be willing to at least give it a try. There is the crux of the issue—the people who gravitate toward unhealthy, violent porn, are people who already have a disposition toward violence. So the problem is not in the porn but the people and what they bring to the table.

Regulating porn access really is going to have no impact on these people as they can (and do) find far more violent and graphic images in mainstream Hollywood "torture porn" films.

Here's some often-ignored empirical science about porn. As societies have increased their access to porn, rates of sex crimes—including exhibitionism, rape, and child abuse—have gone down. **Around the world, and in America, as men have increased ability to view Internet erotica, sex crimes go down.** *Believe it or not—porn is good for society.* This is correlational data, but it is extremely robust, repeated research. However, it's not a message that many people want to hear. Individuals may not like porn, but our society loves it and benefits from it.

It is getting increasingly difficult to find men in our society who've never viewed pornography. But if porn were the problem the problems of porn would be far, far greater than they are. In fact, fewer than 1 percent of people report that they have had problems in their life due to difficulties controlling their sexual behaviors, including watching porn. BUT, around 10 percent of people report "feeling" that their sexual desires are hard to control. It is very different to have a feeling, versus ACTUALLY being out of control of one's behavior.

So, if you are in that 1 percent, what's going on? If it isn't the porn, it must be you. Something about you (more than one thing, usually) has led you to a person who makes poor decisions about sex. Now in that, you're not alone. It is, in fact, a universal truth that people tend to make poorer decisions when

they're turned on, whether it's choosing not to wear a condom or choosing to masturbate to porn when they shouldn't. Call it "sex-goggles," and recognize that human sexual arousal affects our decision making.

But there's more than that going on if you've decided porn is your problem. Here's some more real science about what's going on—you like sex.

Wow, earth shattering, right? Self-identified porn addicts tend to be people with high libido. You are also probably a person who can get turned on very quickly (when you choose to). Further, you probably grew up in a home (or culture) where sex and masturbation were seen as morally wrong.

Having a high libido is not a bad thing. In fact, men (and women) who like sex have changed this world and made it better. Rock stars, politicians, military leaders, and sports stars often tend to be people with high libidos and a high desire to succeed. Sometimes, they actually want to succeed just so they can have lots of sex. Whether we are talking about John Lennon, Catherine the Great, Genghis Khan, or John F. Kennedy, no one can argue that these people liked sex AND that they changed the world. Even Martin Luther King, Jr. was famously recorded by the FBI during sex with various women other than his wife, and Albert Einstein's infidelity was a complex part of his personality and life.

But if you are a man who likes sex, and likes porn, is that something you've ever really owned? I'm sad to say that our society has not taught men how to identify and negotiate their sexual desires or needs. We treat sex like a dirty secret. Then, when men get caught, they feed into that dirty secret mentality and treat sex like it's the problem.

Those other men who like sex, watch porn, and don't get in trouble, how do they do that? One thing is that they understand themselves and their desires. Sometimes, they sit down with their wives and girlfriends and have a real, open discussion about their use of porn, their interest in it, and what it means and doesn't mean about their attraction to and interest in their partner. That's a hard, scary discussion (and not one for the first date, please) because it requires a man to stand up for himself and his sexual desires, to be willing to negotiate for those needs, and to be willing to compromise but stay true to himself, while asking for the same in return.

Another thing about those guys who don't get in trouble for watching porn - they are paying attention to themselves, and are doing the work that is needed to make good decisions. Some men have the Internet or cable turned off in their hotel rooms, or install a net nanny on their own computer so they have less temptation. That's not because porn is the problem but because these men are recognizing (when they're not turned on) that they need to do the prep work, in advance, to make good decisions. It is okay to admit that you make poor decisions when sex or porn are involved. You're not alone in that, and it's not a sin.

But the responsibility is on you to identify why and how you make bad decisions and take steps to make better decisions in the future. When you blame the problems on porn, you're telling yourself, "Porn is more powerful than I am." And I'm here to tell you, that's not true. You CAN take responsibility for your life, your sex, your good decisions and your bad ones, and have the life you want.

Porn's not the problem—you are. But you know what? You're also the solution.

Should You Worry about Porn's Effects?

Like it or not, porn is a big, hot-button issue these days. Sometimes lately I wonder if there was a decision in a back office somewhere, and people said "Hey, we lost the War on Drugs. Let's start a War on Sex!" So much is changing in the world, especially around matters of gender, sexuality, and orientation. These are things that we used to think were simple. Come to find out, they're not. The Internet, and easy, immediate access to information, communication, and private sexual stimulation, has rocked the foundations of core assumptions about humanity. When people are afraid, they lash out, usually at the easiest target. Today, in matters of sex, that's porn. If you watch porn, and you're not at least a little bit nervous about, then you're a rarity. The media, society and modern life is inundated with panic-driven dialogue about the effects of porn. It's okay to worry about it. If you're not a little bit worried, you're not paying attention. But, let's talk about some of the real-world realities behind this panicked dialogue, so you can sort out how much of that anxiety and panic you want to accept.

Is Internet Porn Changing Things?

I met a guy once who aggressively challenged my views. He was sixty years old and told me that when he was a teen, "We had to beat off to the lingerie section of JC Penny's catalogs. Now there's porn everywhere, instantly accessible. You can't tell me there's not a difference and it isn't changing things." I suggested that he forgot to mention about walking uphill in snow to get those catalogs so he could beat off using bear grease as lube.

Of course porn and sexuality on the Internet is changing things. I'm not an idiot. The world is constantly changing. How is porn changing things? Like all technological innovations, from the telephone, the camera, and the automobile, the computer and the Internet have been adapted to sexual uses and have been used to change the way people think about, explore, and have sex.

When post office boxes were invented in the 1800s in Britain, there was a moral panic that these devices might allow women to have covert communication with men and that it would start an epidemic of female infidelity. The invention of the bicycle started a similar panic that bicycle seats were going to turn women into insatiable lesbians. (I will pause here so you can ask your lady to go on a bicycle ride with you. . . .)

Modern silicone lubricant was invented by NASA for smart, scientific things in space. Now it's used in sex and sex toys more than almost any other use. Is that a bad thing? The growth of the Internet, from webcams to P2P file sharing, was driven by demand for pornography. Pornography is why VHS won out over Betamax and why Blu-Ray won over HD.

Every technological advancement results in changes. Often, those changes affect sexuality and sexual behaviors. These changes are never all good or all bad, but we struggle with them, mostly just because they are changes and dealing with change is hard.

Porn and the Internet are no different. What's different these days is that the changes from technology are constant and never stopping. The pace of technological changes is speeding up, with every day bringing new ways to access information and connect with people. These constant changes and inventions are hard for people to deal with, because it's so difficult to keep up with them.

The changes that have resulted from widespread, easy access

to hardcore porn are a mix of good, bad and neutral things. For instance:

- Access to material showing homosexual sexuality has helped many gays and lesbians understand more about themselves and their sexual desires
- The wide availability of hardcore porn has contributed to the increased acceptance of anal sex and is part of the reason why so many people now shave their pubic hair
- People who watch porn tend to be a lot more accepting of different body types, different types of fetish activities like spanking, bondage, or even crossdressing
- People who watch porn are more open to trying new things during sex. People who watch porn are more willing to be "Good, Giving, and Game," when their partner brings up a sexual desire or interest, to use my friend Dan Savage's concept of "GGG."People who are kinky, or have alternative sexual desires, used to keep these desires a dark, dirty secret, under lock and key because they usually thought they were the ONLY ONES who felt this way. Now, the Internet's smorgasbord of porn has shown these folks that there are lots of folks out there with the same interest.

Are these good things or bad things? It depends on your sexual values, your attitudes toward monogamy, sexual propriety, homosexuality, and whether you think kinky sex is inherently a bad thing.

The mystery of sex is gone. Porn did in fact kill it. Back in the day, we didn't know anything about sex, and we would masturbate, looking at lingerie pictures and just imagining what uncovered breasts MIGHT look like. The mystery, the unknown, the allure of the secret was part of the excitement of sex. And now, for many people, there is no real mystery about sex anymore. Want to know what sex actually looks like? Jump on the 'Net and find out in 15.3 seconds.

That mystery of sex was both good and bad though. It was exciting, to be sure. But it also made the first sexual experience for people into something that was usually scary, clumsy, anxiety-filled, and even painful. Pregnancies resulted from that ignorance, as did transmission of sexual infections. Some people romanticize those days, ignoring the pain, fear, and shame that permeated. I'm glad those days are gone, and I celebrate our society moving forward into an era of sexual acceptance, diversity, and open dialogue.

The Gendered Conflict Over Porn

Both men and women watch porn. But more men watch it, and more women fear it.

I'm not going to tiptoe around gender terms in this book. I'm usually going to talk about guys watching porn. I know many women watch porn and might have some of the same concerns about it as men. Women can read this book and get a lot out of it as well, as can trans folks, gender-queer, and a host of other amazing, wonderful people. But men are really struggling right now and getting attacked, vilified, and stigmatized for watching porn.

The debate around porn is an intensely gendered conflict and one that has become morally laden, driven by fear and ideals. There are strong oppositions to porn, fed by extreme statements and by a lot of tiresome arguments about what people and sex "should be," rather than what they actually are. I understand and empathize with the fear and hatred that many women, and some men, have toward porn. The popularity of porn use, especially by men, has become the current battleground of a huge cultural war. People are afraid of the consequences of porn use and fear that it damages men, their brains, their sexual performance, and their attitudes toward women, intimacy, and sex. The dialogue has changed since forty years ago and the days of Take Back the Night, when feminist activists declared that all pornography was rape and should be restricted. Now, porn is presented as a public health issue, involving an addiction that is changing men's brains.

The film *Don Jon* with Joseph Gordon-Levitt tells a different message and suggests that one real problem with porn is not that it is scary but that it is convenient, and offers men a discounted option to the high cost of sex. There is a fascinating subplot in the film, exploring the way sexuality is turned into a commodity. The female lead, Scarlett Johansson's character, uses her sexuality deliberately and blatantly to manipulate Jon's character into complying with her wishes of who he is supposed to be. Scarlett's character flies into a rage when she finds out that Jon has continued to watch pornography. But is she really angry about porn, or is she angry because Jon's easy access to porn takes away some of her power over him?

Social psychologists Roy Baumeister and Jean Twenge wrote a powerful scholarly article where they argued that women actually suppress the sexuality of other women, not men. Their premise was that control of sexuality was historically one of women's only commodities, and that women had to control the market, so to speak, by stigmatizing, shaming, and suppressing those who might offer free, easy, or cheap sex. This is the old argument that women have to defend the value of sex because "nobody buys a cow, if it gives away the milk for free."

I once witnessed a fascinating argument between female sex workers battling over whether sex workers should be able to set a low price for sex, or whether doing so brought down the ability of other sex workers to demand a high rate. I've never before seen this dynamic played out so explicitly. The argument was started by one sex worker, who chastised another woman for "lowballing" her price, which the first woman believed made it harder for get her own prices met. Sadly, versions of this argument play out often, though usually masked by one woman calling another one a "slut" with no explicit reference to money.

Women are taught to suppress their sexuality. When they see another woman reject that teaching, it triggers an internal conflict, where they start wondering and fearing what it might be like if they also started to express their sexual desires. Even women in porn can trigger that conflict, making a woman struggle with her own internal shaming about sex. Women in porn love sex and have lots of it. Some women want that too and hate themselves for wanting it.

At one point in *Don Jon*, Jon says that "real" sex is less satisfying than porn and masturbation because during sex with a woman, "it's on me to do all the work." But, during porn, Jon can sit back, watch for free, "lose himself" in the fantasy of porn, and not have to work. He can be selfish with his sexuality.

Because porn is free and convenient, Don Jon can relax and focus on himself, exploring his pleasure rather than maintaining a focus on the needs of his partner.

That sexual freedom is frightening to many because there is a cultural value that sex isn't supposed to be free, easy or casual. Sex, according to the current anti-porn narrative, is supposed to be costly—expensive in both effort and emotions. It is supposed to involve intimacy and emotionally transparent connection. Don Jon, like all men, has been subject to a society where sex is constantly held out on the end of a string in front of them, and a man is told to work like a horse to earn that sex. The high value of sex has been programmed into men, women, and our culture. It doesn't have to be this way.

Our society is starting to celebrate and empower female sexuality now with Slutwalks and feminist activists embracing their ability to like sex just as much as men. Some of these activists watch porn, and some make porn. Perhaps these women can change the gender battle over porn and sex, from being about control and fear of sex. All of a sudden, women who rely on control of sex for their power and value have a new, powerful threat on the market.

Because all of a sudden, men don't have to work that hard to get sex, or at least a reasonable simulacrum.

Internet porn is not just a cow that gives away the milk for free, but creates a world where milk simply gushes out of a tap in the bedroom at the mere click of a mouse.

The Effect of Being "Pornified"

Sometimes men who watch a lot of porn find themselves thinking about sex and thinking about women they see in sexual ways. It's easy to blame this on an effect of porn and to argue that porn has "pornified" these men, warped their brains, and turned them into scary perverts who walk secretly amongst us, "undressing women with their eyes."

This is one of those catastrophic things that people blame on porn. But, I had a hobby for years, collecting old 1950s Popular Science magazines. In the back of those magazines, right next to the ads for how to get muscular so beefy guys wouldn't kick sand in your face, were ads for "X-Ray Vision Glasses." We all know what those were for. Decades before the advent of the Internet, young men around the country wanted to be able to put on special glasses and sneakily see the naked bodies of their neighbors, teachers, schoolmates, and their older sisters' friends. Those old-style X-ray glasses didn't actually work. They just created a fuzzy halo around people's images. But, nowadays, for about a thousand bucks, you can actually buy goggles that do appear to perform this magic trick. Or, you can simply get online and see the pictures made by people who use photo-software filters to create images that appear to see through the clothes of celebrities.

But people don't want other people walking around, "objectifying them," and seeing them in sexual ways without consent. And porn use is blamed for causing this. At its core, this complaint about porn is worried that porn teaches men to objectify women and see them as nothing more than sex "objects."

Nobody wants to be seen as merely an object. We all want to be seen as a person, a unique being, with our own thoughts, feelings, needs, and desires. But, as usual, sexual objectification is, for some reason, treated as especially "wrong" compared to other types of objectification.

Our society, in fact, thrives on objectification. You don't think telemarketers REALLY care about you as a person, do you? Objectification is not necessarily a bad thing. Surgeons commonly "objectify" their patients because it is easier to cut into them when the surgeon is not distracted by thoughts of this person's feelings, future and past. Soldiers objectify their enemies to make it easier to attack or kill them. What do we tell a person who is afraid of public speaking? "Imagine your audience naked. . . ." (However, having presented to naked audiences, I can tell you that, in fact, I still had anxiety, though it was definitely of a different sort. . . .)

Research with pornography and objectification has actually shown that when we see someone as a sexualized "object," there are some good sides to that. When we are sexualizing someone,

we tend to see them as someone who experiences things in a powerful way. We see them as "experiencers," who we can imagine "experiencing" sex with us. There was an old study years ago where people thought they were giving electric shocks to other people. Current studies on sexual objectification suggest that if that person were showing more skin, or was even naked, people would shock them less. Not because they want to get laid by that poor person, but because we believe, on the basis of that sexual objectification, that they would feel the pain more intensely than other people.

Imagine that you are at an outdoor concert, and the bright sun is shining right in your eyes. But, oh joy, the lady right in front of you is wearing a big sun hat. Before, you were annoyed because the hat blocked your view. But now, you move slightly to the side, and the sun disappears behind her hat. You just objectified that poor woman. You just treated her like she was nothing more than an object that you could use for your selfish convenience. You selfish beast, you.

But during sex, there is a cultural ideal that you're not supposed to objectify someone. You are supposed to be connecting with their soul and their heart, and sex is supposed to involve an intimacy and a joining. When that happens, it is beautiful, wonderful and amazing. But this is a cultural ideal—one that reflects a division between common gender values toward sex. Men typically see sex in more pragmatic, casual, less emotional ways than most women do. Men are more prone to objectify others. It's something that is seen in male leadership and communication styles and in masculine sexuality. Rejecting this has more to do with disagreeing with aspects of masculinity and less to do with porn.

In fact, human sexuality and sexual relationships are based on objectification. When we are attracted to someone, that initial attraction is usually a physical one, based upon their face, body, smell (yes, their smell), and physical appearance. Hopefully, as we fall in love with someone, we see them as more than just their external appearance.

During sex, there is a moment when a person must surrender to their own body, to a selfish focus on their own orgasm, their own pleasure, and allow those sensations to wash across them. We might urge our partner on, telling them to keep doing what they're doing so that we cross that brink and let our orgasm take us away. When we do so, we are objectifying our partner, treating them for a moment as merely a means for us to achieve orgasm. We are being selfish for an instant. And then that moment passes, and we cuddle, chat with our partner, and/or return the favor. Right? (If you're not returning the favor, or trying too, then regardless of your gender, you ARE being a selfish asshole and porn is the least of your problems.)

That moment of objectification passes. This is the important part. There's a fear, in ourselves and in others, that if we are walking around sexually objectifying others, we might not be able to stop. We might turn into ogre rapists, filled with overwhelming lust for others, taking what we selfishly want without regard for the needs of others. But, if you are constantly objectifying and hurting people, it's because of a lot of other things, not just porn. It's not because you were "pornified." There are ways to address this, though, by looking within ourselves rather than at porn. In a later section, I discuss ways to manage unwelcome sexual thoughts, through that self-understanding and acceptance.

Your Brain on Porn

There has been a tremendous amount of panicked hyperbole about porn use, with doomsayers claiming that viewing porn triggers dangerous neurochemical changes in the brain. It is raining porn, they say, and the sky is falling. But research says that it just ain't so, and the brains of people who are high users of porn look like the brains of people with high libidos, NOT people whose brains have been warped by sex and porn.

Popular anti-porn advocates claim that if people and society only knew the damage that porn use was causing to our brains, we would regulate it, in ourselves and in the access that is allowed. This isn't a new strategy. The Temperance Movement, which led the 1919 prohibition of alcohol in the United States, claimed that science was behind their efforts, and that public health was at risk from alcohol. Those who opposed alcohol blamed it for all manner of things, including crime, mental illness and poverty. But, after alcohol was prohibited, those social problems all still existed.

What is new in these arguments against porn, is the invocation of our new national obsession: brain science. Over recent years, these fear-based arguments against porn invoke brain-related lingo and throw around terms like dopamine bursts and desensitization to describe what allegedly happens in the brains of people who watch too much porn. Brain science is hot these days, and it's attention-getting to use brain and neuroscience lingo in arguments because it sounds so gosh-darned convincing and scientific. The problem is, there has been extremely little good research that actually looks at the brains and behaviors of people using porn, and our understanding of the brain doesn't really justify lots of these conclusions.

Many anti-porn folks have claimed that porn is the "crack cocaine" of sex. The phrase "your brain on porn" is reminiscent of the "This is your brain on drugs" failed antidrug campaign of the '80s. I call this Valley Girl Thinking. Some people think that saying something is "like" something else is convincing. But an apple is "like" a banana, right? Except that one is red and the other is yellow. You can eat an apple's skin but banana peels taste like shit. Apples come from trees, and bananas grow on big plants. So, are they really "like" one another? Does that even mean anything? Come on, gag me with a curling iron. Let's leave the Valley Girl Science in the '80s where it belongs. Argument by analogy is just rhetoric.

The latest ploy in this arena is to argue that porn today is equivalent to tobacco in the '50s, when people didn't acknowledge the health effects of cigarettes. I point out to these people that six million people died worldwide last year from the effects of tobacco—how many died from porn? Umm. Zero? Tell me more about how porn is like tobacco.

The brain is constantly changing. Anything we do repetitively changes aspects of the brain, whether it is watching lots of porn or playing Sudoku on your phone—this is in the nature of neurology. There is no ability of any of this research to distinguish porn-related change from any other brain changes constantly occurring.

The brains of people who watch lots of porn may actually be different from the brains of people who don't like porn. But the difference isn't in the porn. It's in their brains. The brains of people who like sex and who need a higher level of sensation and experience to get excited appear to be somewhat different from the brains of people who don't like sex and don't need much excitement in their lives. Some people like to race motorcycles, and some people prefer to drive a station wagon. Some of the differences in what makes these people unlike each other can be seen in their brains.

People who like lots of sex and lots of excitement may actually have slightly smaller brains and slightly less reactive neurochemistry. What this means is that these people need MORE

stimulation to get satisfied and to have fun. Their thresholds are higher. So that's why they think skydiving, or group sex, is a blast where the same activity might be just "too much" for other people.

But, sex or porn didn't make these people (I'm talking about you here, by the way, just in case you weren't listening) this way. Your brain was already like this, whether due to biology, or your life, or both. You've ended up as a person who likes porn, sex and sexual excitement because of the brain you started out with.

Every few months lately, a new research article is published, looking at brains on porn. But none of these research studies have yet looked at "causality," and whether it is actually porn that causes these brain changes or whether these brain issues were already there. They also have not compared the brains of folks who watch lots of porn to the brains of people who watch lots of television, or to people who just have lots of sex or masturbate a lot, without porn. Until they do, these brain studies are mostly just another ploy of people who want you to be afraid of porn.

Currently, attempts to identify neurochemical pathways for sexual or pornography addiction are, at best, speculative, according to leading brain researchers. Right now, and for the foreseeable future, the brain remains a complex, multi-determined "black box" that we are just barely beginning to understand.

The role of the brain in complex behaviors such as sex promises to be a riddle for many long years to come. When we solve the riddle, the answers will not be simple ones, as they will have to account for all factors including the brain, human behavior, learning history, evolutionary influences, environment, free will, and sexual desire.

I like to reference the story of Chicken Little, who believed the sky was falling. This is an incredibly old story, thousands of years old, and tells a core truth about humans, and fear. Chicken Little fears the sky is falling, and gets other people to panic. They are invited into a cave by Foxy Loxy, who promises to protect them from the dangerous world out there. But the fox then eats them. When people tell you to be afraid, in an ambiguous, unclear situation, you need to wonder why they want you to be afraid, and what they intend to do with that fear of yours.

Blaming Porn for Bad Sex

You can't turn around these days without hearing claims that porn is teaching men to behave like oafs in bed. Aside from the ludicrous, antiquated claims that porn turns men into rapists or pedophiles, there is a genuine social outcry that young men are getting into bed and expecting "porn sex." There are articles, TED talks, websites and more, all complaining that men are learning bad behaviors from porn. When I talk about sexuality and research on porn, I often hear complaints like this email I got:

> From a woman, on the "front lines," porn is most definitely damaging to men of all ages. I'm thirty years old, and every time I sleep with a man, it seems they are trying harder and more painful acts with me, and this

is all as a result of porn. Guys are definitely more sexist than they were when I was twenty, and I have no doubt that this is due to being inundated with these hardcore, degrading images. They also make the men enjoy sex less, less likely to please, and more displeased with me (and I am attractive by any standard).

Sincerely, Laura.

On behalf of men everywhere, I think guys who behave this way in bed with a woman are idiots. A man who acts like this has never been taught to be a gentleman and is an insensitive lout who needs serious help understanding relationships, sexuality, communication, and how to have a reciprocal experience in bed.

However, I'm skeptical of the degree to which porn is a scapegoat. It's a distraction and a simplistic answer to blame porn alone for these problems. Women have been complaining about young men in similar ways for millennia, chastising them for being too eager, too rough, too clumsy, sexually ignorant and for not paying enough attention to foreplay or to women's sexual needs.

Despite the fact that most gay men are consumers of porn, I've not heard or seen this complaint expressed by gay men about their male partners' behavior. This suggests to me that the real complaint here is an age-old issue of sexual communication and reciprocity between men and women.

In 1918, Marie Stopes wrote a sex education manual, *Married Love*. In it, she discussed the common unsatisfying sexual experiences of women who don't understand their own sexuality, as they marry men who are equally ignorant of female desire and pleasure. She suggested that women need to anticipate, and be prepared to deal with, the fact that some men may come to marriage carrying misconceptions they learned from prostitutes. (Interesting side note—Stopes' book was banned for decades as obscene, and the book triggered a moral panic that it encouraged women to enjoy sex. The book is also referenced in the popular show *Downton Abbey.*)

Today these problems are blamed on porn. But, it takes two to tango, doesn't it? If a woman is going to bed with men who behave in disrespectful, insensitive ways, she might be with the wrong men. A guy who can listen, empathize with a woman, be respectful and treat her with dignity over dinner and a date, will probably behave the same way in bed. If he gets excited and carried away because of lack of experience, these same skills will help him to listen and understand when the woman talks about her needs and desires. When I suggested this to Laura, I got a fascinating response:

> I am a forward-thinking, progressive woman who is in touch with her sexuality. I feel like I am taking a step backward if I have to be a gatekeeper of sex, which is what you are implying. But yeah, I guess I can try to go all 1950s and get a guy to wine and dine me. Might be the only solution at this point.

There's a fantasy here too. Laura seems to think that in today's modern world of feminism, a woman's needs should be automatically met in bed and she shouldn't have to be a "gatekeeper" of who she has sex with. I'm sorry, but a woman has to be just as personally responsible as she wants men to be.

In Marie Stopes' manual, she recommended that education, personal understanding and insight are critical to have satisfying sex and relationships. The central component she describes is "mutuality," or give and take. Both people having sex have to be aware of themselves, their own needs, and be ready to talk about those needs with their partner. Laura needs to learn mutuality is a two-way street.

Good sex doesn't happen by magic. And when it doesn't—it's not porn's fault.

Former porn star Jenna Jameson says, "When it comes to being a good lover, a guy has to ask a girl what she wants and be willing to give it to her." I will add that the woman also has to be willing to answer the question.

BOTH people in bed are responsible for themselves and for communicating with their partner. This is one of the key points missing in most porn. Most porn conveys a fantasy that earth-shattering sex can occur without communication, without undue effort, and without a whole lot of thoughtfulness or insight (romance literature and romantic movies typically present the same fantasy, in less graphic ways).

Good, ethical porn often includes video prologues and epilogues to their videos. In these before and after clips, the performers first describe what they were looking for in their sexual experiences and then talk about what felt good during the onscreen encounter. This process is, in fact, an exceptionally good model for healthy, mutually satisfying sex.

If your partner does

something you don't like, or doesn't do something you do like, and you never tell them, your unhappiness is your responsibility. If you keep going to bed with people who don't listen to you, it begs the question of whether you really want someone to listen or feel like you deserve to be heard. Let's stop blaming porn for being the fantasy that it is and instead encourage people to take personal responsibility for the health of their relationships.

The Fear Industry and How It's Hurting You

HUSTLER Magazine's Larry Flynt has an interesting book where he speculates on the media's obsession with sex and scandal. In it, he describes the changes in media over the last twenty years. The days of detailed investigative journalism are sadly gone. Today's media thrives on what Flynt calls "gotcha" journalism, which succeeds by being first to promote a story and by getting a larger number of people to click, listen or watch, a story, no matter the accuracy or value of the story.

One clever and insidious strategy the media uses is to instill a sense of inferiority and anxiety in a viewer. By sparking fear, insecurity, and tension with that headline, teaser, or commercial, they're hoping that enough people will follow the rest of the story to relieve that fear. Otherwise, we might go through the rest of our lives wondering, "Am I a good lover? What if I'm not? I SHOULD have read/watched/listened to that story!"

Part of the problem here is that our media thrives on instilling fear and inadequacy in people. They want you to be afraid, to feel anxiety, so that you read their article or watch their television show, all so they can sell you shit via advertisements and commercials. Fear about sex and health are two of their main strategies.

But let's face it, our parents' generation and their medical advice has been wrong about a lot. They told us that eggs were bad for us and that we should take multivitamins every day. It turns out that multivitamins don't do a damn thing and eggs, including the yolks, are actually really healthy. When the media is constantly filled with these moving targets, changing messages, and fear-based strategies, should we really be listening to them anyway?

Think for a minute about all the varied sex scandals involving people who were public advocates against sex, homosexuality, porn, and prostitution. Politicians, ministers, and activists, caught doing exactly the thing they were railing against. It's easy to say these people were just hypocrites, but I think it goes deeper than that. I don't think they are truly conscious of this conflict between their words and their actions. At some level, they believe that the only way to stop themselves is for society to stop them.

People who advocate against various forms of sex and porn are in fact asking us to understand that they are afraid they cannot control their sexual desires. They don't seem able to hear us when we say that we too sometimes struggle with our sexual desires, but that this is human and understandable. It is clearly something where their fear is far worse than the thing they fear, and the energy they give to their fear only heightens their panic. Unfortunately, their fear has filled the media, which exploits sexual fears and anxiety.

A young man once called to see me, telling me that he was twenty-two years old and he'd been masturbating to porn since he was fifteen. He was "ready to deal with his porn addiction," he told me. We scheduled for him to come in. He said, "Oh yeah, by the way, while I'm there, I guess we should also maybe talk about the heroin I shoot up most weekends." Seriously. This is the damage being done by a fear industry's obsessive focus on sex.

You don't have to be afraid of your sexual arousal, or even that of other people. We fear things we don't understand. That's why my goal for this book is to increase your understanding of your sexuality and the reasons why you respond the way you do. Then, you can look at these people with pity and feel sorry for them, rather than letting their fear and panic infect you.

Porn & Your Relationship

The first place where problems with porn use surface is almost always in a man's relationship, usually with a woman. Is porn use damaging to the relationship? Is masturbation to porn a form of infidelity? Whether it is or isn't, it represents a threat, and a challenge, to many ideas about monogamy and love. Most women know their guy has looked at porn, but most men never really talk to their women about what porn means, or doesn't mean to them. As a result, porn creates a minefield for men in relationships. A minefield that they can only navigate if they begin to explore their partner's idea about porn, and communicate about their choice to use porn.

Is Watching Porn Cheating?

Watching porn is, or could be a form of cheating, if you haven't ever talked with your partner about it.

Most guys don't admit to their wives or girlfriends that they still masturbate and look at porn. The wife might suspect, might even have a "don't ask, don't tell" approach. Until she turns on the computer and you left up that page with the gangbang video. And it all comes crashing down.

We will talk much more about how to talk to your partner about your porn use. But for now, consider something. One of the biggest problems with modern relationship ideals is the belief that the perfect relationship has no secrets, no barriers, and nothing stands between you and your partner. This is a fairy tale, as we all know, because people don't actually work like this. We're not made of glass.

In the fairy tale relationship with no barriers between two souls and minds, communication is unnecessary because the two people share one mind and have no differences of opinion, seeing everything the same way. In fairy tales, the prince and princess live happily ever after. Until the princess gets on Facebook and finds out the prince friended an ex-girlfriend. Until the prince goes out with the guys and finds out the princess danced with a guy at a club during her girls' night out and hadn't told him. Until the mortgage for the castle comes due, and the prince's job gets laid off, or the mother-in-law comes to visit and never leaves. And the fairy tale comes crashing down.

In the real world, we have to talk about things and find ways to respect each other's opinion, even when we disagree. A healthy, mutually satisfying relationship involves celebrating the things you love about each other and ignoring, whenever possible, those quirks that you can't change.

When it comes to sexual behaviors, there's a belief today that there should be absolutely no privacy between the partners in a couple. That any privacy is the equivalent of keeping secrets, and that secrets are unhealthy and destructive. But healthy sexuality and a healthy self involves some privacy. If you choose to exercise your sexual privacy and watch porn, you should be able to.

Just like your partner doesn't tell you that she sometimes thinks of other guys (guys she knows or met—women usually fantasize about people they know while men typically fantasize about unknown or even faceless people) during sex, you have the right to some healthy degree of privacy in your sexuality as well. It may be different from hers, but it is just as valid, healthy and valuable.

You can tell her that you watch porn sometimes, and that you hope she can deal with that, because you really want to have a healthy, open, mutually accepting relationship with her. But, if you tell her that you don't watch porn, when you do, then you're lying, and perpetuating your shame, and her misunderstanding of porn. Lies don't earn privacy—honesty and integrity do.

Talking to Your Wife/Girlfriend about Porn

Can you really blame women for hating porn? Think about the programming and constant messages that they've gotten that lead them to believe porn is dangerous and immoral, and interferes in their relationships. Look at all the ways that porn can affect women negatively:

- The idea of porn can trigger women's concerns about their body image (a fear programmed and promoted by an exploitative media) and their need to compete for male attention.
- It can make women feel that they need to compete with and be compared to porn performers.
- Women believe they have to be prepared to compete with porn fantasy sex, and be just as sexy, orgasmic, sexually open as porn performers.
- Women have been told that they have to worry about porn performers being taken advantage of, sex-trafficked, or coming from abusive backgrounds.
- Women worry about social judgment if people knew they watch or tolerate porn. Women who don't reject/judge porn are seen as sluts.
- Women worry about you becoming "pornified" in bed and wanting to have anal sex all the time.
- Women worry that your interest in porn means that you don't love and desire them like a princess, which means that you won't live happily ever after.

We need to empathize and understand a woman who fears or hates porn. She didn't really have much of a chance to see it any other way. Hate the social programming and the "control through fear" tactic. Don't hate the person.

Many women I've seen in therapy have told me that the porn only really becomes a problem when it is paired with what feels like rejection of her. "*You stopped wanting sex with me anymore and left me with my needs unmet while you were off with porn!*" So, women are concerned that porn might result in them losing out. Women know that men have looked at porn. The days are gone when women could believe THEIR boyfriend or husband didn't look at porn. Today, women know that you have looked at it. But the problem is usually rooted in the woman's belief that while he has looked at it, he's not looking at it NOW. That you have looked at it in the past is one thing. But looking at it now means something more. It might mean, to her at least, that she is not enough for you.

That you are looking at porn now, while you are still in love with her and able to have sex with her, is a different ball of wax.

So think strategically about your goal. What do you want her to know? Ultimately, you want her to know and accept that sometimes you watch porn, but the porn doesn't change your feelings about her. And really, the porn is a part of your private life, which you'd like to be able to share with her and not be shamed or judged.

So, try:

- Asking her if there are private things that she worries about telling you for fear you will reject her. This is a chance to support and accept her and then share your use of porn.
- Asking her what she thinks of porn. But you need to salt the mine a bit first. If you ask flat out, you will get the politically

safe answer that it's bad and she thinks it's stupid. If she answers otherwise, she might worry you would judge her, or that if she is too accepting, you will turn into a porn fiend. So plant some seeds first, like mentioning the kinds of porn you dislike or that you dislike porn stars who seem fake (or fake orgasms, or whatever).

- Acknowledging that you've watched porn in the past and being prepared for the question about current use.
- Thinking in advance about how you can reassure her that you find her attractive and sexy, that porn is not more important than her, and that watching porn doesn't change you or your feelings about her.

You CAN take the stance of, "This is something I choose to do and has nothing to do with you. I'm telling you I watch porn just so you know, not because I'm giving you permission to have an opinion about it." Some guys do this. But, chances are, you're not one of them. And, this strategy doesn't build on the empathy and understanding I'm arguing for. Those things can make your relationship stronger, using a discussion of porn to strengthen its foundations.

How to Talk to Her about Watching Porn with You

Lots of guys would really like to watch porn with the women they love. But women often resist and feel like it's too much to ask and a "bridge too far," even though they make their men suffer through romance movies galore.

Here's the thing, you may not be able to get her to give porn a chance. And, if you push it, whine about it, beg and plead, you become obnoxious and self-sabotaging, fucking it up for yourself and the rest of us too.

Here's one tip. Allison Vivas wrote a great book—*Making Peace with Porn: Adult Entertainment and Your Guy.* Buy it for your lady. It opens a woman's eyes to her fears of porn and what the realities are in her relationship with you.

But when you want to talk to her about watching it with you? Remember in the movie *Grease*, when Danny says to the other guys, "Be cool!"? Dude, if you want your girlfriend to watch porn with you, you gotta be cool.

You can't argue a person into it. Remember, she's been filled with the idea that porn involves harm, is exploitative of others, and of sex in general, and that after watching porn, you will want to enact on her everything done in the porn.

Should you ask her about it before sex or after? Either way, it might lead to her being concerned that you are somehow saying she "isn't enough" and the sex you are getting ready to have, or just had, would be so much better if porn was involved. That sounds like a giant trap filled with punji sticks of porn. (Punji sticks were bamboo spears, coated with feces, used as traps during the Vietnam War.)

My suggestion is that this topic works best as a part of a broader conversation between the people in a relationship about how sexuality works in themselves and in their relationship. "I love you, and I love our relationship. I love making love to you, and I wonder if we could talk about our sex life and how it's working for you. I think it would be fun if we talked about ways to do some different things in our sex life, and I wonder if there are things you're interested in as well. I'm not suggesting that I'm in any way dissatisfied with our sex life, but one of the things I love about our sexuality is when we have fun with it together."

It'd be best if you were so cool about it that she made it her idea to watch porn with you. If she does, make sure you stay cool. If you get all hyper about it, overly excited again, you'll screw it up for yourself.

If she does decide to watch porn with you—here are the rules:

Number One—Let her drive. Make sure she understands that you're going to let her control the experience. She can switch or stop videos, she can initiate or stop sexual activity between you two. If she likes the experience and wants to repeat it, she can, but you aren't going to pressure. (Many guys ruin this experience for themselves by pressuring their partners to watch porn, making it about themselves, not her.) Think of yourself as a tour guide, out to give her a pleasant experience, see some nice scenery and some things she might not see at home.

Number Two—Before jumping in there and whipping out

those hardcore gangbang Ass to Mouth videos you've been excited about, remember—this is her tour, not yours. So start by asking her what she is interested in. Is there a type of porn she might like to see? Are there things she DOESN'T want to see? Be mindful and thoughtful about where you take her on this trip to Pornland. Sure, she might like to see the gutters, ghettos, and dive bars, but more likely, you want to save that for a future trip. Lots of porn websites have "couples," or "romantic," or "female-centered" categories. These can be your friends. Nice places to start. (And relatively very safe, from a risk and ethical standpoint.) If she finds it tame, let her drive the bus and explore around.

Number Three—It's her trip here, brother, not yours. Don't focus on your arousal. Focus on hers. Ask her what she likes as she's watching. Tell her that it turns you on for her to enjoy it. Make it safe for her to experience and express her arousal. Tell her how beautiful she is and how beautiful her arousal makes her. If she gets turned on enough to have sex, remember Rule One. Let her drive. If she wants to keep the porn on or is ready to turn it off and jump your bones, Rule One says that's her prerogative.

Finally, it's important and useful to process afterward, acknowledging and allaying any of the above fears, shames, guilt, or concerns that might come flooding in once those sexy hormones start to subside. In other words, tell her that you had fun. If she wants to do it again sometime, that'd be cool. But you don't want to do it every time. Be cool, bro.

Trying to Prevent Infidelity by Fighting Porn?

I've noticed an interesting dynamic in men who come to see me for porn, sex, or infidelity problems. For these guys to stay in their marriage, they have to give up all privacy. They give their wives all their passwords, let her control their phone, and spend a lot of time being "transparent" about where they are and what they're doing. The guys usually are desperate to stay in the relationship and to prove they've reformed and can be trusted.

I understand where they're coming from and the questions those wives are wrestling with. Lots of people believe that watching porn leads to people cheating on their marriages, getting so worked up about sex that they go and find a prostitute, a bathhouse, or an adult video store with gloryholes, just to get some sex. Under this theory, preventing porn watching makes sense. At least it would if this theory were true. Unfortunately, there's not a shred of research supporting it.

In fact, using these efforts to control your spouse, prevent them looking at porn, or being tempted, might actually increase their desire to pursue extramarital sex.

Research on this shows that trying to control someone's sexuality actually makes them more dissatisfied with their current relationship, decreases their commitment, and increases their interest in pursuing an extramarital relationship. It also increases how much attention the people pay to other attractive people and how well they remember them.

I call this the "forbidden fruit syndrome." By telling Adam and Eve not to eat that damn apple, God created a burning desire to have what they couldn't have and essentially destined them to break his commandment. I tell wives and girlfriends that by trying to prevent their spouses or partners from cheating or watching porn, they might be creating the same effect. By setting and enforcing limits, they are almost certainly increasing the men's unhappiness with them and their relationships, AND they might be making the men more likely to start shopping around for alternatives.

I remember a couple I saw years ago, where the wife was convinced that her husband would one day cheat on her. By telling him repeatedly that she already didn't trust him and believed he would cheat, she led to him eventually saying in therapy one day, "Why shouldn't I cheat? She already believes I will. I'm already paying the price for the crime I haven't done. I've really got nothing to lose."

When you put your spouse or partner on notice that you are "watching them like a hawk," what you are really doing is telling them that they need to be prepared to better hide their actions and desires because you don't trust them.

What's a better way to deal with this situation? With that couple I treated, I encouraged the wife to instead spend a lot of time paying attention to those qualities of her husband that she admired and respected, which would increase his internal barriers to infidelity—things like his moral character, his commitment to her, his desire and love for her, and the joy they had being together. Want your spouse to be faithful? Here are a few tips that actually work:

- Be clear about what faithfulness means. Many problems happen due to lack of clear communication about expectations and agreements.
- Talk about porn use. Is all porn bad? Are there types of porn that are okay? What about erotica? Why do you fear porn, and are there things you don't like about porn? Knowing what those things are might help your man make decisions that don't hurt you, or might help him to help you understand what porn is and isn't for him.

- Help your partner to want to be faithful by having a healthy relationship. That doesn't mean you should always keep them happy, but you should do your part to communicate and deal with problems.
- Pay attention to the things that are working. Often people in relationships only attend to the things that aren't working, which enhances awareness of dissatisfaction. Instead, we do best by highlighting things we like even more than the things we don't. "That which we attend to grows."

- Deal with your own fears and feelings over infidelity. What does it mean to you and your beliefs about yourself and your relationship?
- Talk about it. Guess what, talking about it with your partner doesn't make it happen. Instead, talking openly and honestly about the issue of extramarital sex and desire with respect and personal ownership of feelings helps you and your partner make better decisions about your relationship, commitment, and reactions to those "attractive alternatives."
- And sometimes, developing sexual tension through mystery, through secrets and excitement, is just what the doctor or-

dered. Sometimes, a couple needs to learn to fuck each other like they are fucking a stranger and cheating.

Rather than making them not cheat, make them *want* to *not* cheat through having a relationship where they feel no need to do so. Make that forbidden fruit less desirable, less mysterious, and less alluring than yourself.

Consider the radical idea that porn use probably DECREASES infidelity far more than increasing it. Lots of guys watch porn, and take an edge off their horniness, and this might prevent them ever "stepping out." In the US, there is a huge, lucrative industry that lives off the fear, problems, and issues related to infidelity. They'll sell you books, websites, television shows, counseling, legal representation, and mediation around the issue of infidelity. Like so many things related to sex, people want you to be afraid of infidelity, and they are blaming porn for it because it's an easy target.

But it's likely that men who use porn to get that thrill, that sexual novelty, that sexual excitement within their long-term marriage may be less likely to cheat because they can scratch that itch without leaving the house, breaking the marriage agreement or touching another woman.

Here's another radical idea—instead of preventing infidelity by trying to prevent porn use, prevent infidelity by making some hot, homemade personal porn together. In both men and women, infidelity is often related to a desire for adventure and excitement to feel sexy and desired. Homemade porn can be an exciting adventure to explore together.

Choosing Porn over Sex

There are men who choose to watch porn and masturbate rather than having sex, even when they have a woman who wants to have sex with them. And you know what? **There might be nothing wrong with those men.**

There is an outcry over wives who want their husbands to screw them, but the man is instead watching porn. Sometimes these wives are called "porn widows," like porn dressed up in a trench coat and went and put out a hit on their husband. Way to catastrophize—porn didn't just affect the husband's sexuality, it went all *Goodfellas* and put a .22 caliber bullet in his brain!

There's an implicit assumption in here that we should examine. That assumption is: A real man, a healthy man, always wants to have sex. And would always choose real sex over masturbation.

Let me ask, if we changed the gender in that statement, would you agree with it? A real woman, a healthy woman, always wants to have sex. And would always choose real sex over masturbation. I suspect not. Because we can imagine many times when that woman is healthy and doesn't want to have sex:

- We can imagine times when she's angry with her man and doesn't want to have sex with him, but she's still horny.
- Maybe she worries about her body and whether he finds her attractive, and that gets in the way during sex but not masturbation.
- Maybe she is more attracted to people of the same sex and has more difficulty getting turned on because her husband's body doesn't match what she is aroused by.
- Perhaps she has secret kink desires, fantasies of being spanked, tied up, or of being in charge and treating her husband as her slave. But she has to keep these fantasies secret

for fear that her husband will judge or shame her for them. Or even more likely, she has shared the fantasies with her husband, and he did shame her for them. When watching porn depicting those desires, she can allow herself to relax and enjoy the fantasies free of that fear of rejection and shame.

- Maybe she has physical pain, and having sex is daunting because of the risk of hurting. During masturbation, she can prevent and avoid pain in a way that is tough with another person involved.
- We can even imagine that her husband is a pretty bad lover, can't make her come, and that sex with him is just really a frustrating waste of time.

For any or all of these, sure she would want to "flick her Bic" or "paddle the man in the canoe" rather than have sex.

Can those same things be true of a man? If not, why not? They are only true of men and not women, IF we are assuming some very biased, sexist attitudes about men.

Throughout this book, I talk about the complex, multi-varied ways that men use porn and masturbation. I acknowledge the many different functions of masturbation and porn. Masturbation and sexual intercourse are NOT the same thing. They do different things. Masturbation is not merely a substitute for sex (though sometimes it can be). As a human behavior, masturbation has its own value, role, and function.

Writing this book, I've thought a lot about my own life and my own sexuality. Years and years ago, I went through an incredibly stressful period of my life. It was early in my marriage, very early in my career, and I was under excruciating personal pressures. At work, there were unbelievably stressful personality conflicts, and on top of that, there were financial pressures in my life. Ultimately, I was stretched so thin that I worried I was simply going to pop.

My wife and I have a great marriage and a great physical relationship. But that period is one where she remembers that I often chose to watch porn and/or masturbate rather than have sex. Looking back, with wiser eyes, I can say that sometimes I simply didn't have the emotional resources for physical intimacy. But I didn't know how to say that. And I certainly didn't know how to negotiate that in a way that my wife didn't feel rejected.

To put it simply—yes, there are normal, healthy times and reasons when a man, or woman, might prefer to masturbate versus having sex. Masturbation to porn can be a stimulating, easy way to get your mind off of things that are bothering you or stressing you out, things that might get in the way of you being mindful enough to have good, mutually satisfying sex.

For folks with mental or physical disabilities, masturbation to porn may be a completely healthy and satisfying part of their sexuality if they are socially isolated, as so often happens.

None of these things are about the porn. They're about the person and what role masturbation plays in their life. Sometimes, a good porn-fueled masturbation session is exactly what the doctor ordered.

Porn, Marriage, and Divorce

I am often forced to respond to claims that porn is bad for marriage. In Utah, a state senator called on the state legislature to condemn porn as a public health issue and, specifically, as something that was "destroying marriage." According to this resolution, porn was somehow causing infidelity, destroying marriages, AND was leading young men to not want to get married.

As I spoke publicly against these fairly ludicrous claims, I kept getting hit by a certain statistic. According to research, porn is now involved in over 50 percent of divorces in our country. Oh my God! Porn IS destroying marriages! I will admit, every time I got hit by this number, it threw me for a loop. Then a skeptical friend of mine did some digging and uncovered some interesting facts about this Porn Destroys Marriage statistic.

The origin of this lies with two groups. First, the Family Research Council has asserted that they conducted research and found that porn was involved in over 50 percent of divorces. But the FRC is a conservative activist group founded by James Dobson, which promotes "traditional family values" and lobbies against divorce, pornography, abortion, gay rights, gay adoption, and gay marriage. The FRC's study of pornography and divorce was not published in a research journal or subjected to peer review. We have no reason to believe it's a valid representation of marriage in America.

The second origin of this mysterious panicking statistic about divorce and porn is from The American Academy of Matrimonial Lawyers. In 2003, at one of their conferences, the Academy did a survey of 350 attorneys. About half of these attorneys reported that they had seen online porn play a part in divorces (but they didn't say they'd seen porn in 50% of divorces!). Again, this survey has never been published and these data never analyzed. We wrote to the Academy and requested information on this survey, but never heard back. These results have never been replicated in further studies.

So, does porn cause divorce? I gotta tell you, I don't think anybody actually knows, or can know. In 2015, I conducted a study where we examined legal records from across the United States, looking at cases where pornography or claims of sex addiction had been involved. There WERE lots of cases where claims of pornography use or porn addiction were involved in divorce or custody hearings in family law. But, it's really tough to find these cases and even tougher to find out just how much porn was ACTUALLY involved. I remember one case where the wife accused the husband of always watching porn and that this was why they had to divorce. But then, during the court hearings, she admitted that she had watched porn with him many times in the past but then decided she didn't want to anymore. And when she was asked, she couldn't actually describe times that she found porn, or found her husband watching it, but she was just SURE he was. So, was porn involved in their divorce? I guess so, but porn seems like the least of the issues here.

Remember, divorce is an adversarial process. It is two people, once in love, now battling over who gets the toaster. If one spouse has cheated, the other spouse and attorney will throw that out there as a way to diminish the cheaters' credibility. Porn use is another great way to make the opposing spouse look slimy to the judge. So, the fact that porn may be getting raised in the midst of divorce hearings means little.

Published research has looked at the effect of porn on marriages and relationships, and the effects are complex and not so simple as saying "porn causes divorce." When a husband watches porn in secret from his wife, there are also often problems in the relationship. But those problems probably aren't caused by the porn. Instead, the secret porn use may be a symptom of the conflict in the marriage, as one partner is going to porn for sexual satisfaction or as a way to deal with loneliness or sadness in a marriage that is struggling. In marriages that are disintegrating, it makes sense that lonely, depressed men gravitate towards porn. Couples who watch porn together, or where both watch porn separately, are about as happy as couples where neither one watches porn. Couples who watch porn tend to be a bit more adventurous and willing to explore different types of sexuality—from oral to anal to sex toys or bondage behaviors. So, these couples are likely to have better developed communication skills, acceptance of each other's sexual needs, and negotiation around sexuality. It's not clear that porn is a cause of these things, and it's more likely that sexually healthy, open people, can have healthy, honest relationships and deal more effectively with porn, and other issues.

When wives watch porn, their relationships are healthier, whether the husband knows the wife watches porn or not. This might be because the relationship is more accepting of sexual expression, or sexual privacy, and it might just be because a woman who watches porn is more likely to have a higher libido, and women with higher libidos tend to have happier marriages on average.

If a husband or partner is watching porn and the wife knows it because the husband was "caught," the wife is more likely to report that her husband is less interested in sex with her. This might be because of the porn. But, it might just as likely be that the husband doesn't really want to have sex with her and is using porn as an outlet.

If you are a man who is watching porn in secret from your wife, then you and your porn use could hurt your marriage. But it's not the porn—it's the fact that you're in a marriage where your porn use is something that is unaccepted, by you, your wife, and often your therapist, pastor, and community.

In the end, porn doesn't cause marriages to divorce. Problems that come up in a marriage or divorce are caused by the people involved in the relationship (including those therapists, pastors, and communities that tell you what's healthy or not) and their assumptions about sex, communication, privacy, negotiation, and whether each other's sexuality "belongs" to the other one, like sexual pleasure is a form of property. When porn gets raised as a problem in the marriage, it's always a symptom of something going on with one of the people in the marriage, or in the marriage itself.

Stop Watching Porn and Get a Girlfriend?

There's a generation of guys coming along now, who have been watching porn for a long time but have never had sex with a partner. Some of them are concerned that porn is actually getting in the way of them being motivated enough to get a date and have some "real" sex. They worry that porn has made them lazy.

Look, sad fact for you if you're one of those guys. Chances are that you probably would have had a lot of trouble meeting or talking to a girl, before the days of Internet porn. Guess what— in the time before the Internet and porn, there were lots of guys (and girls) who had trouble meeting people or talking to the opposite sex (or the same sex if that's what they were interested in). Those folks went home alone, felt left out, and were lonely and sad. They maybe had books or role-playing games or music or chess club (to be clear, as a kid, I sucked at music but was a kickass chess player and had a seriously high level half-elf D&D character) to entertain or divert them. They didn't have porn available, for better or worse, but they still felt deprived, ignored and sexually starved.

Porn didn't create loneliness or social awkwardness. In fact, it might have offered guys a solace, an escape and outlet, which many past folks didn't have when they were lonely. Maybe, just maybe, because you've been able to masturbate to porn, that easy substitute made it so you didn't have to push yourself, to improve yourself, to be someone attractive to girls. Maybe. Or maybe you are who you are today just as you would have been without porn.

For some reason, many guys have the idea that there is something wrong with them, if they haven't gotten laid and don't have a girlfriend. Maybe there is. Maybe they have rotten dirty-shoe breath. Or maybe getting relationships and having good sex is a lot harder than we all really want to acknowledge. On television and in movies, it looks so easy. Meet "the one," fall in love, have great sex, live happily ever after.

There are lots of people out there just like you, who feel awkward with people they're interested in, who don't know how to talk to people or how to try to be attractive. This is why the Pick-Up Artist (PUA) community/industry exists because there are so many guys who feel just like you do, and they wanted to learn how to meet girls and get phone numbers.

I'm not encouraging guys to pursue the PUA strategy. I neither hate nor love what they do. I understand where they are coming from. They said, "Why can't we just learn how to do the 'secret right click, left joystick push-push A button cheat trick' that gives us the invincible power in this game of meeting girls?" They'd like to be able to have multiple lives and chances for do-overs instead of suffering shame and embarrassment when they flub trying to meet a girl.

But I think there's something a little shallow in their strategies, and they treat other people rather poorly. It doesn't feel very gentlemanly. Instead of learning how to be themselves, they're learning how to pretend they are something they're not. Ultimately, I think that's self-defeating if you are so ashamed and embarrassed of yourself that you want to be someone and something else.

Stop focusing on porn as your problem, and start focusing on yourself. Who do you want to be? What kind of man do you want to be? If you try to expand and explore who you are, oftentimes, that is attractive to other people. So grow yourself and accept that maybe you are one of those many wonderful people who don't peak till they're in their twenties.

How to Start Having Sex Again Instead of Watching Porn

I often hear stories about men who have been watching porn for years and have gotten to the point where they prefer watching it and masturbating to having sex with their wives. I've treated some of these couples, and of course the issue isn't really about porn. It's about relationships, sex, libido, negotiation, and the fact that, sometimes, relationships can lose that sexual spark. Regardless, these men sometimes (but not always) want to start having sex with their wives, and they want to want sex more.

First, don't expect this to be easy. There's no magic pill or process that is going to make a man prefer sex with his wife if he's spent years developing a sexual arousal and response pattern to porn.

Over the years, I've seen a surprising number of couples like this, who just kind of fell away from having sex with each other. In some cases, decades go by. The really sad, difficult thing is when the couple does want to have sex, but there are these barriers, these speedbumps, they can't get over. These couples

have been some of the most challenging I've ever worked with because the inertia of not having sex has built up, such that getting them to just start trying is like pushing a boulder up hill—a boulder with years' worth of grass and moss weighing it down.

If you want to start having sex with her and want to enjoy sex with her as much or more than you enjoy masturbating to porn, you've got to do two things:

1. Start having sex with her.
2. Figure out what you like about masturbating to porn and try to incorporate those things into sex with her.

Simple, right?

Seriously. #1. Start having sex with her. Remember, you get to write your own definition of what sex is for you and her. It doesn't have to involve putting your penis in her vagina. So, start with backrubs, you performing oral sex on her, mutual masturbation. If you feel like you might not be into it because you're forcing yourself (a recipe for having difficulty getting an erection), this is when you decide to have sex with her that doesn't involve your dick. Ask her, "If we had sex, and I didn't use my penis, and I didn't even care if I came, what would you want me to do?" But, don't let the inertia stop you. You have to push through.

#2. There are reasons why you might like porn more than sex with your wife. And it's not because of the porn. You might enjoy the novelty that porn offers, something that sometimes goes comatose in long-term relationships. Or maybe sex with your wife is challenging because she doesn't seem to enjoy it, so that porn is a chance to relax and be selfish. Whatever. It's your job to figure out the things that make masturbation to porn so appealing and brainstorm how to bring them into sex with your wife. If it's novelty, then figure out how to bring novelty and excitement into your sex life.

Notice how I didn't say you should stop watching porn. You might choose to. Or might not. I don't think it matters. Sex with your wife is something different from masturbating to porn. The two things can and should inform each other. Learn from them in order to better understand yourself and your own sexual needs.

If you don't find your wife sexually attractive anymore, it's time to start asking some hard questions and exploring what's going on there. It might be normal aging and the developmental staging of relationships. But it might not, and maybe you're choosing porn for reasons related to that. Stopping porn isn't going to make you magically horny enough that you suddenly become attracted to your wife. It doesn't work that way.

Erections to Porn vs. Sex

I've seen many men who are concerned that they get hard easily when watching porn, but when with a sex partner, it takes them longer. Men get worried that this is ERECTILE DYSFUNC-TION and there's few things that are scarier to a man than their dick not working when they think it should. But what's going on here isn't anything bad, and isn't really because of porn.

Look, when you're watching porn, you're alone, like most men when they watch porn. So you can relax, focus on yourself, and seek out something that stimulates you. But when you're with your girlfriend, it's a very different experience. Granted, the differences are often wonderful and amazing. But sometimes, the differences are work. The famous saying is, "Hell is other people." Bringing other people into sex changes things. Sometimes in good ways. Sometimes in hard ways.

When you're having sex with someone (as opposed to solo sex—aka masturbation), you can become preoccupied BE-CAUSE YOU CARE about your partner's pleasure. And that's a good thing! Your own pleasure waxes and wanes in intensity, and your signs of physical arousal (aka your boner) may reflect that. Your self-worth might be tied up in whether or not you can make a woman come.

So guess what—that little question, and a thousand other mental nagging anxieties, can slow us down. Those things can get in the way of getting an erection. And for the most part, these types of anxieties aren't present when we are jerking off to porn.

When we sit down to watch porn, we are in more of a receptive, passive mode. That's very different from the active role we need to take when in bed with a woman. Even if she's taking the lead, we sometimes worry about getting hard, about whether she's enjoying herself, whether her jaw is getting tired, etc. We don't have to worry about whether the Internet is going to have an orgasm!

In romance novels and movies, men's erections are treated as an external symbol of the man's passion. Some even call it the "pogo penis phenomenon." In the real world, men's erections are influenced by many different things, from what we just ate to what's happening at work and what our last sex encounter was like. Our cocks are not some kind of "Love Lie Detector."

If anything, getting hard quickly with porn and less readily with your girlfriend means that you really are taking sex with her seriously, and you want her to enjoy herself. Tell her (and yourself) not to worry. You've got fingers and a tongue until your dick decides to relax enough to get hard.

That's the funny paradox of erections. You have to relax to allow yourself to get an erection. Physiologically, your body has to relax blood vessel constriction to allow blood to flow into the penis and create an erection. Psychologically, you have to relax enough to let it happen. It's like the saying, a watched pot never boils.

I recently had a chance to interview a man who had been a leading voice for the NoFap community (an online group who oppose "fapping" or masturbating to porn) and published several popular articles in mainstream media about how porn addiction had changed his brain and caused erectile dysfunction. Through luck, I tracked the man down two years after he'd written those articles. He wasn't writing about porn addiction anymore, and I asked him why?

He told me that even though he'd not watched porn in two years, he still had problems with ED. He was now starting to think that his ED had more to do with anxiety, and the moral conflicts he had about sex. As a result, he was no longer crusading against porn or blaming it for hurting his erection. He still felt like porn was an important issue to deal with, and that there were lots of people struggling with it, but he was realizing now that porn wasn't actually what had caused his problems. I wish more people could hear that and think that way. Maybe then they would stop spreading fear of porn amongst men, and help these young men to consider some of the more subtle issues in their lives and sexuality.

To Send a Dick Pic or Not?

If Shakespeare wrote Hamlet today, he wouldn't be asking "To be, or not be?" He'd be asking, "Should I send Ophelia a dick pic or not?"

Essentially any woman who has EVER ventured into the world of online dating, or almost any form of modern electronic communication, can tell you that men routinely send them pictures of their genitals. Women complain about this for two main reasons:

- First, they really don't want to see these pics.
- Secondly, guys send the pics without asking, often without any explanation or context. Often, sending such a picture is one of the first communications women receive from these men.

When you talk to women about this, "Men are GROSS," is the most common explanation that they have. Some others might add, "They're GROSS and STUPID. Do they really think I'm going to magically want to have sex with them now after seeing their penis?"

As silly as this issue might seem to be, it offers some genuine opportunity for insight into the ways that modern technology reveals interesting aspects of sexuality and gender. This is definitely more of a guy thing. At least, in terms of sending the pictures unrequested. Both males and females are commonly sending nudes of themselves to people they meet online, but women tend to wait until asked. That difference might simply be an expression of gender differences in mating and dating strategies. The fact is, women are told that being sexually bold in such a manner is shameful and makes them sluts.

There aren't any research studies looking at this question, and so all we can do right now is speculate with some informed psychological wisdom:

- It is likely that this behavior represents men's misperception of female sexual interest. Men love the idea of receiving such pictures from strangers, and they assume women do too. Men notoriously overestimate women's sexual interest in them, and project their own sexual interests and desires onto women. In this situation, men really are hoping and thinking that a woman will be turned on and send them a naughty pic in response.
- Some of this probably connects to the fact that in an anonymous environment, people, and especially men, are likely to engage in more sexualized behaviors. Psychological research has demonstrated that in anonymous environments, people, both men and women, engage in fairly casual sexual behaviors, including exhibitionism.
- Male mating strategies have always included an element of "boldness," where men who are bold and brash sometimes garner female attention they wouldn't otherwise receive if they were nice and polite. This is a key tenet behind Pick-Up Artist strategies, where men are encouraged to be bold and impulsive. So, "shock value" is a way for men to get attention. And negative attention is better than no attention at all.
- It's probable that at least some of these men get a sexual thrill at the idea of an unknown woman seeing their dick. It's an aspect of exhibitionism, and some of these men probably masturbate as a part of the act, imagining that woman seeing

the picture they sent. The fact that a woman rejects them for it is not important because for many such men, the woman's disgust and rejection is actually part of the turn-on. These are the same types of men that used to be in trench coats on street corners.

- Men fear sexual rejection, and by sending pics of their dicks, they are getting "pre-approval." This way, they get the chance of rejection out of the way early, so they don't have to worry about being rejected or shamed once they drop their pants on a real date.

Within gay male circles, this behavior is very common and isn't a problem. In fact, lots of gay men are happy to get such pictures and usually respond in kind. That's important because it offers some confirmation that many men want to receive such pics and are really hoping their recipient will enjoy it and be turned on. But for many reasons, women don't enjoy this the way men do.

Men have gone to jail over sending dick pics to underage persons and have ended up as registered sex offenders. If you are sending these pictures to people you don't know, they might turn out to be underage.

A lot of women are genuinely bothered by this behavior and view it as an unwelcome intrusion. Some writers have described this as a form of sexual assault and a way in which men assert the dominance of their sexuality over that of women. I can see the point, and I empathize with women who are offended and grossed out at receiving such images.

Ultimately, the answer here lies in greater dialogue with men and women over what they actually want in sexual communications. This MIGHT help some of these men to stop offending such women, when those men are genuinely not understanding that most women don't want to see their dicks. But this requires women to actually have the safety to be honest about their sexual interests. It would be nice if women could say, "Look, I probably WOULD like to see your penis pic, but I'd like to be able to ASK for it. . . ." That would give us all hope that at some point, they will ask for it, and get turned on by it, and send us a similar picture back!

Unfortunately, I don't think such dialogue is happening, or even possible right now. People who are offended and grossed out at such images would like them banned. They want men to understand that such behaviors are rude and unacceptable and should simply stop. Women have tried attacking such men, flaming and shaming them, both online and in personal communications. Some women love the idea of sending a response like: "It looks like a penis, but smaller. . . ." But such strategies probably won't work.

A basic premise of psychology is that punishment is still a form of reinforcement, which gives energy to something. The more uproar, outrage, and disgust that such pics get, the more powerful some men feel. They are proud that their penis generated this strong reaction. So, shaming, banning, flaming strategies are unlikely to be successful. A better strategy is to ignore it. I know that probably feels unsatisfying to women who are frustrated at this. But if they remove the reinforcement, including negative attention, some of these men might view this behavior as ultimately unrewarding.

So—if you're the guy sending these pics, it's up to you to think about why you're doing it. If you're thinking it might turn on the woman and she will send you back pics of her tits or ass, **think again**. I know you'd like it if they did send a pic. We all would. But it just won't happen anytime soon. And as long as you keep sending the pics of your cock, hard or not, big or not, women aren't going to feel safe ever saying that they kinda do enjoy the idea of seeing your dick. They just want a chance to be in control of the experience.

Invite Her to Make Homemade Porn with You

Some guys really would like to act out the porn they watch, and even better, make porn themselves. I'm seeing this more and more these days, as people are developing their sexual identities in response to porn. It makes sense. If you've learned about your sexuality, and what turns you on, by watching porn, then acting out porn is one way to culminate that development.

Being a porn star in their own private production is a common fantasy among men and women who watch porn. Sex, and the desire to make your own porn videos, was one of the main reasons why VHS tapes and home video cameras were so successful. Recording your kids' birthday party was just the reason you justified getting that video camera—we all knew what it was really for.

If you are wanting to make sex videos now, there are lots of options, and I understand your desire. It seems like everyone's doing it, from rock stars to reality stars to high school kids. But, if you want to be ethical about it and safe from legal problems, here's some tips:

First, be over the age of eighteen! There is a bizarre conflict these days, where people under the age of eighteen can legally consent to have sex. But, these same people cannot legally consent to have naked pictures of themselves or share them with other people. Countless teenagers have been charged with having and distributing child pornography, for having pictures of themselves. The battle against child pornography has led to criminalizing children themselves and creating arbitrary laws that limit teen sexuality from engaging with technology until age eighteen. So, assuming you are eighteen plus, your desire to make porn videos and pictures makes perfect sense to me. Sex on screen is a way to engage your real life with your fantasy—with your ideal of sex. It's like becoming a sex star.

How do you invite your girlfriend/wife to do it with you on video? Think first about the concerns she will have:

- It will get released publicly and ruin her life.
- She will look ugly or unsexy in it.
- Making it will make her into a slut, a whore, or a porn star. Or, will make you think she's one of those things. Maybe she wants you to treat her that way on film because it feels sexy and naughty, but she's probably worried that you might treat her that way all the time, in ways she doesn't like.

So, be prepared to talk to her about ways to make this experience safe, fun, and sexy. There are easy ways to make such videos where it's not recorded but merely displayed on screen. So, you position a camera so that it shows on screen what you are doing. Then the two of you have sex while watching yourselves on screen. During it, you tell her how sexy she looks, how beautiful she is, and how much she turns you on. This might be enough to satisfy your fantasy and desire—"Look, there you are! Fucking! On screen!" If not, it might help her to become more comfortable with the idea of making a recording. . . .

*Here's a tip—pay attention to lighting! Better yet, spend some time researching "How to make your own amateur sex video." Even better—make it a team project and do the research together.

But whatever you do, don't make a sex video of her without her permission. That's the reason for revenge porn laws. It's also the way that lots of awful rapists get caught. I'm glad they are so stupid as to record themselves committing sex crimes. We shouldn't have to work very hard to prosecute them, lock them up, and protect people from them. By recording and posting such videos, they make it easy. And talk to her about what you do with the porn if you guys should break up. And don't be a dirtbag and screw it up for the rest of us by posting it online without her permission. Don't be a dick.

Porn,

Fantasy,

and

"Real Sex"

One of the biggest problems with the debate over porn, is that people seem to forget that porn is just a fantasy. Like Hollywood blockbusters, porn films depict things on the screen, that we wish were real, or could be real. Talking with porn superstar Chanel Preston, I was delighted when she shared that she loves to know what's in peoples' heads, so that she can bring their fantasies to life on the screen. People have always had sexual fantasies that they didn't, couldn't, share with other people. But porn lays those fantasies bare, for the world to see. Our fear of porn has more to do with our fear of sexual fantasies, and of the power of sexual pleasure. But, when we've not thought clearly or well about what porn is for us, most of us cannot clearly distinguish between our fantasies, porn, and what our real sexual life is. Sadly, when generations are robbed of the benefit of sexual education, they have no framework to understand or distinguish porn, fantasy, or real life sex.

Masturbating to Porn vs. Using Your "Sexual Imagination"

I've heard from many men and women, who are concerned about themselves or others, who use porn EVERY time they masturbate. They worry that if you only EVER masturbate to porn, you will at some point become dependent on porn for your sexual arousal. The argument flows from the core value that the best, most ideal sex is between two people and masturbation is merely a substitute. There's the belief that too much substitution can ultimately damage "the real thing."

For some people, even many people, masturbation may be

their main form of sex. Some prefer masturbation over sex and don't view sex with another person as their ideal. If you're one of those people, then making porn a regular, consistent, and reliable part of your sexuality has little to no risk of impacting your sex life.

Some people crave regularity, consistency and predictability in their lives, including their sex lives. Long-married couples often have sex in exactly the same way, even on the same nights of the week, year after year. Every person is different, and while this unceasing, consistent repetition might be unhealthy for some people, for others it's not.

How can this consistency have an impact, even if it isn't unhealthy? Merely through the effects of behavioral conditioning. Pavlov trained dogs to salivate at the sound of a bell by consistently pairing food with the sound of the bell. The dogs' learned that bells meant food. Those couples who are extremely consistent with their sexual routine might struggle to get turned on if the routine changes. In the same way, by constantly pairing porn and masturbation, it could create the effect that you might not get easily turned on without porn.

If you were stuck on a deserted island, or if the Internet suddenly broke, you might find it a little difficult to masturbate without porn, at least at first. But, Pavlov's dogs stopped salivating after a while when the bells rang and rang, and they got no food. This type of conditioning is not a permanent thing. It's not "rewiring" your brain, not in a lasting sense anyway. On that deserted island, your sexual imagination would have to get exercised again, and you would get better at it. (Good luck making some lotion from coconuts.)

The one issue that I can see is that people who constantly rely on external material for arousal are not exercising their own sexual imagination and not exploring the erotic fantasies they can create in their own brains. I don't know if there's anything truly unhealthy about that, but many people look at it and feel like there is something lacking. I feel the same way about people who only watch television and never read a book. I might disagree with it, but to call it unhealthy is a stretch.

I know a guy who's an artist. He's never, ever masturbated without either porn or pictures of nudes. As a teenager, when he couldn't get porn, this creative fellow would draw a picture of a nude woman and then masturbate to it. It's hard for me to call that unhealthy, or to argue that it is somehow the result of porn. Instead, it shows how creative he was in using his mind and talents to fulfill his sexuality.

I think that exercising your sexual imagination is healthy and a way to be in charge of your own sexuality. Porn puts us in a more passive state of mind around our sexuality. I think it's why women can feel slighted, or even ashamed, if a guy wants to act out what he saw in porn. In bed, people usually want a partner who is present. Having someone say, "Be like a porn star," is the worst form of "objectification" and really treats your partner as a sex toy. Sometimes that's sexy, but often it's not.

Let's face it—it's sexier and hotter to say, "I've always had this secret sexy fantasy, which I would love to be able to try to act out with you." Compare that to, "I saw this hot thing in a porno last night, and I want to do that. Watch this porn and let's do it!" Both could be fun and sexy, but when you share a fantasy from your mind, you're revealing a part of yourself. Saying, "Let's do what was in this hot porn," is the equivalent of saying, "Hey, watch this funny cat video on Facebook."

Porn Sex vs. Real Sex

Some porn-obsessed men are treating their female partners like porn stars, and spoiling things in bed. Real life and porn are dif-

ferent. In porn, things are easy. Women always say yes. Everything anyone does feels great. Penises get hard all the time, lubrication is automatic and orgasms are everywhere. At least the porn finished product looks that way. The behind-the-scenes reality is a lot more work. A lot more preparation, both in terms of lube and communication. Real life sex looks more like the behind the scenes world of porn. Hopefully with fewer pauses for adjusting camera angles.

What happens backstage making a porn video involves

communication, discussion, negotiation, and dialogue. Onscreen, a guy might shove himself in a girl's ass with no preparation or asking. Offscreen? The performers had already said that anal was okay, lube had been applied, and everybody knew that anal penetration was coming.

The key difference is in the communication, negotiation, and mutual respect. Maybe your girlfriend wants to be slapped in the face with your erection. It happens a lot in porn, and some women do find it sexy and arousing. But many don't. You don't know which one your girlfriend is unless you ask her.

Maybe you say, "So sometimes, in porn, I think it's really sexy when the guy just grabs the girl and sort of throws her around and really takes her. I think that might be sexy to do sometime. What do you think?"

So long as you are okay with her saying, "Hell no!" Or okay with her saying, "I think it's sexy when the girl shoves her foot in the guy's mouth and makes him go down on it. Would you be interested in playing like that sometime?"

People in porn treat each other like objects, but offscreen, that was all negotiated. In real life, you can do the same, but you have to include the offscreen parts as well.

Jerking Off to Porn vs. Having "Real Sex"

Jerking off to porn isn't as satisfying as real sex, is it? Is it? This is the way the question is treated on daytime talk shows and romantic-comedy movies. Porn is fun and all, but it's not as good as the "real thing." Porn and masturbation are just wasting time compared to "real sex" with another person. These are the implicit ways the conversation about porn use is usually framed.

Why does this have to be framed as an either-or question? Why are masturbation to porn and sex framed as being in opposition? Is there a competition between them? Is the devil on one side and angels on the other? That's the way it's framed, right? That sex in love is godly, idealistic and beautiful. Jerking it to porn is base, brutish, and, at best, a tolerably necessary evil.

And why is it assumed that your answer to which is better is always the same? Are there times when an orgasm from masturbation might feel better, more fulfilling, than an orgasm from sex? Aren't there times when a wonderful, conjoined, emotional, soul-connecting kind of sex feels wonderful and other times when we like it hard or aggressive or selfish? Most people enjoy sex in a range of ways. No one way is better than the other. They just fit differently, in different people, at different times.

Sometimes masturbation to porn might feel better than sex with a partner because it's a time when we can be relaxed, focusing on our own pleasure. We can explore our own fantasies and physical reactions. Masturbation to porn might allow an exploration of deeply fulfilling and desired fantasies in a way simply impossible in real life.

There's an assumption that an orgasm from penis in vagina sex is the best kind of orgasm. But some guys have trouble coming from that or from oral sex. Some women can't orgasm from sex, but need clitoral stimulation or from a vibrator. We've mostly stopped judging and condemning the quality of those female orgasms, haven't we? Women who need clitoral stimulation during sex in order to orgasm are told that they are normal, that this is just part of biology. But if a man needs to masturbate or look at porn to get erect, there's something wrong with him?

I like to tell a story about a man I once interviewed, whose only sexual outlet was masturbating to porn. He could ONLY get turned on by a very specific type of porn. He would masturbate to it, and then he would cry. Sounds sad, right? Poor guy. Geez, porn really is messing this guy up.

But here's the rest of the story: his wife died from breast cancer a few years ago. They were married for decades and loved each other deeply. The porn he watches is porn he made with his wife. Now it's not sad, it's just bittersweet and "pornomantic."

Let's just say that masturbation is a form of sex and orgasms from masturbation feel good, and so do orgasms from intercourse. I'm just happy with all of them and thankful that Mother Nature or a benevolent God gifted us with them. Same with ice cream. I love all the flavors, and I don't think there's something wrong with you for liking vanilla when I like chocolate cherry.

Male vs. Female Sex Fantasies

Lots of people believe that women are better than men at keeping their sexual fantasies under control. This is one reason why male sexual fantasies are seen as much scarier and worrisome compared to women's fantasies. Guys are seen as impulsive and sexually obsessed. Ultimately, men are seen as less sexually trustworthy.

In the 1970s, writer and feminist Nancy Friday published groundbreaking books which exposed the secret sexual fantasies of women. These women were normal, everyday people, but their fantasies were anything but the prim, proper, "normal" fantasies that society expects. Instead, these normal women fantasized about group sex, incest, rape, domination, bestiality, exhibitionism and every other flavor in between. The extraordinary success of the book *Fifty Shades of Grey*, driven originally by the safety of anonymously and covertly being able to read the tale as an e-book, reveals that women are still drawn to erotic fantasy that is taboo and forbidden. E-book sellers know this—popular erotic e-books, sold primarily to women, contain wild plot elements and sexual behaviors from gangbangs to sex with monsters like Bigfoot.

But no one tries to ban these books, arguing that Bigfoot needs to be protected from hordes of horny women descending on his lonely cave and forcing him to ravish them. Male fantasies, however, are painted with a different light. When Nancy Friday published a follow-up book of male sexual fantasies, she described that she often felt dirty after reading them and would literally wash her hands after handling the letters. In Britain, pornography and film clips that depicted fantasized rape were banned and prohibited in 2013, with the explicit justification that doing so would prevent men from pursuing these fantasies.

This is the view of men held by society at large—by men, as well as women. Movies, television shows, commercials, fiction, *Cosmopolitan Magazine* stories and *Playboy Magazine* jokes all depict men in this way: unable to control themselves when turned on. Women are seen as being able to have perverse, disturbing fantasies but not act on them. Men, however, are seen as impulsive, weak beings who can be easily controlled and overwhelmed by their sexual desires. The same fantasies are deemed unsafe for men because men can't be trusted to keep them merely in their heads.

As a man, I resent this. As a psychologist, I reject it. I've seen both men and women who hold frightening, disturbing fantasies and never act on them. And I've seen both men and women who acted out, in real life, their destructive secret thoughts. There is no difference between the fantasies of those who act them out and those who do not. Fantasies don't really tell us anything about the person who has them. There are very healthy, normal-looking people, from grandmothers to surgeons, who hold frightening, twisted fantasies in their heads.

The fear of male sexuality and male sexual fantasy may be well-founded, or at least understandable. Men are seen as "doers." There is a long social history of male sexual privilege, where rape was often excused or swept under the rug. Men are, on average, more physically powerful than women, and thus, are seen as being better able to force their fantasies upon another, bringing them into reality. But this fear is based on assumptions and intuitions. I fear that it can be a self-fulfilling prophecy. If we tell men they can't control themselves, we shouldn't be surprised when they choose not to.

Men have just as much ability as women to think and fantasize about things but never do them. Our behaviors and choices are based on many other factors, not just our fantasies.

Watching Transgender Porn Doesn't Make You Gay

A surprising number of straight men enjoy porn featuring transgender performers. This is another thing we've learned about male sexuality, thanks to the Internet and the availability of a wide variety of porn. (The terms "shemale," "chicks-with-dicks," and "tranny" are offensive to many trans people. So, I use the term "TG" for transgender porn.)

Many in the sex addiction industry stigmatize the trans community, and treat their attraction to trans people as though it is a disease. One therapist in California advertises that he specializes in helping sex addicts with "tranny issues," as though a transgender person is themselves a drug. Talk about objectification!

But, if liking trans porn doesn't mean someone is gay, and doesn't mean they're sick, then why do straight men like TG porn? We don't really know, but here are some theories:

- Writer and researcher Ogi Ogas has argued that transgender-porn may contain a complex combination of triggers and cues for arousal, working together in unique ways. This theory is interesting and clever, but doesn't explain why some men like TG porn and others don't.

- Men who go to TG sex workers are most often "straight" or "bisexual." Interestingly, the straight men have said that the thing they like about the TG sex workers is that they are raunchy, funny, coarse, and laid back. They act aggressively toward the men, complimenting them on their looks and the size of their penis. A Twitter friend of mine is a TG porn star named Bailey Jay. She is beautiful, and proudly makes porn showing her hard penis. She is raunchy and ribald, whether she is commenting on sex or politics. In short, some trans MTF people act a bit more like men when it comes to sex. For many men, that sexual freedom and confidence is sexy and fun, and the same effect might be present with TG porn.

- There is a "novelty" factor. Some porn distributors have found that a successful marketing strategy is inserting a few different, but related types of porn on other pages. The unique kind stands out by its difference, and many men click on it, just because of that difference. This is the, "Huh, I wonder what that looks like effect." Interest in novelty is normal, not a sign of illness or disease. Buck Angel is a studly porn performer and producer. He's muscular, bald, covered in tattoos and usually smoking big fat cigars. And oh yeah, he's a trans male who markets himself as "The Man with a Pussy." Buck is an amazing, kind and thoughtful man who has made his sexuality into a powerful part of his identity.

- If you're watching TG porn, you might actually not be as straight as you might like to think. Maybe you are a "tad" bisexual, or just sexually fluid in ways. In fact, many people have aspects of bisexuality or sexual fluidity in their life. Many gay men and women have had opposite sex encounters. Many straight people have had occasional same sex encounters or fantasies. The "strictly" straight or "totally" gay person is actually a rarity.

Many lesbians watch gay male porn. The porn people watch may not really tell us much about their identity, which is impacted more by society.

Men can be sexually fluid, and explore different aspects of their sexuality. The anonymity of porn on the Internet lets them break out from the rigid mold imposed on male sexuality. Watching TG porn isn't hurting anybody and probably doesn't mean anything. Relax, and enjoy.

Why Men Want a MFF Threesome but Watch FMM+ Porn

Men fantasizing about having a threesome with two women (MFF) is the most common, universal fantasy of Western men. It's so common that the fantasy is regarded as normal in media and conversation. "Well of course he fantasizes about that, he's a guy," is often the assumption.

But in thinking about this fantasy, we've hit on an interesting issue in the world of Internet porn. It is in fact dominated by porn that shows a single female having sex with multiple men (FMM+). Given that most porn is designed for men, we would expect there to be more of a focus on the MFF threesome. Right?

There's research that points us toward one possible answer—sperm competition. When guys watch porn with multiple guys and a single female, they ejaculate harder, their ejaculate contains more sperm, and the guys get hard again faster.

Sperm competition theory is an idea that our sexuality evolved in a sort of arms race between males and females with both of our bodies competing for conception and reproduction. Some male rats have sperm that actually act as "killer sperm" and go after the sperm of other males if other male sperm is present in the female's vagina. The strong response that human males have to porn with these signals of "competition" (i.e., other men's penises and sperm) may have come from this process.

In other words, in a gangbang, if you want to reproduce and get that female pregnant, your sperm are really going to have get in there and fight. The more sperm you can get "on the playing field" the better.

(It is worth noting that this archetypal situation was likely a rape, not a consensual group scene . . .) So, it's likely that such porn is very effectively triggering these built-in signals to our bodies that ramp up the male sexual response system and make our orgasms more powerful and get us even more turned on.

The thing that I find really interesting about this is that makers and distributors of Internet pornography hit on this phenomenon by accident, through the free market economy. Because more men gravitated toward such FMM+ type porn, came back to it more frequently, and watched it for longer, porn producers started making more of it. In the process, they helped us discover a hidden part of male sexuality. Who says porn never does anything good or hasn't contributed anything?

Rape Porn and Rape Fantasies

I've seen both men and women who struggle with their interest in watching violent, aggressive porn—videos that simulate rape.

Men worry that their reaction to this material means they could actually be a rapist, which makes them feel guilty. Women worry that liking such porn means they're a traitor to other women, or that they are somehow encouraging men to rape them and even excusing rape.

Rape porn is a controversial, challenging issue. In many areas of the world, it has been explicitly identified as potentially illegal. This material is often extremely graphic and is the stuff that is most often held up by anti-porn activists as representing misogyny and hatred of women. Such porn that is made outside the United States, or that is amateur, can sometimes be real rape and not simulated. As a result, it may very well be illegal in almost any jurisdiction.

The risks are great and not just related to its legality. Getting caught or exposed watching such material brings great risk of public shame, stigma, and judgment, almost as bad as if you get caught watching child porn. It could affect you and certainly is likely to affect women in your life and how they feel about you.

One porn star, Belle Knox, a famous starlet college student, did one of these videos for a very graphic site. During it, she was demeaned and treated very aggressively. Belle has said in interviews that she'd not do it again. But she said doing that work was important for her, and doing that scene was part of her choice in order to work through some issues about herself. She is clear that she was in charge of herself and her choice to do it.

What does that mean? It means that sometimes, women are struggling with these issues as well. Many women, up to 60-75 percent, will admit enjoying fantasies of forced sex, depending on how the question is asked. A smaller, but still significant percentage of men admit to fantasizing about rape. So, fantasies and interest in this porn aren't uncommon.

What does the rape fantasy mean? Lots of things. And perhaps in that, it means nothing. Our society romanticizes rape and violence in complex and disturbing ways, from the Beast pounding on Beauty's door in *Beauty and the Beast* to the content of thousands of romance novels, where women "swoon" and "succumb" to male passion and dominance. Fantasies of forced or rough sex may, in some cases, be the result of social programming.

When I see someone who feels a conflict, liking something they feel badly about, there's often anger, sadness, hopelessness, and fear connected to this, and those are valuable things to explore. Not every guy who likes watching extreme bondage/rape porn is angry at women or afraid of them. The answer to the question of why they feel these ways and what they're doing about these feelings then becomes an important issue to explore.

Watching such porn, simulated or real, CAN increase the chances of a man engaging in such acts if he is already disposed to violence, regularly uses drugs or alcohol (lowering judgment and impulse control), and is angry towards women (or a specific woman) and not dealing with it. If this describes you, you shouldn't watch such material. But, if you are a woman or man who watches rape porn, and worries about why it turns you on, rest easy. You're not a budding rapist or rape victim. You're just human.

Extreme Sexual Fantasies

Sometimes people watch extreme porn or engage in sex fantasies that feel really scary. The fantasies may feel more frightening when they look at them in the cold light of day, when they're not turned on. That fear can easily convince them that their secret fantasies are more messed up than anyone else's. And it's easy to worry that if anyone else knew, they would know how screwed up you truly are.

But here's the thing about that fear: ***You're not the only one.***

By far. At a deep, almost universal level, everyone is worried that they are way more screwed up than everyone else. Some folks call it the fraud syndrome, or the impostor syndrome. Basically it is that fear that you are faking it—you don't really know what you're doing and don't belong where you are—and at some point, people around you will figure it out.

Throughout my career, at parties, on planes, in cabs, and on the sidewalk, when people find out I'm a psychologist, I invariably get one of two responses: "Gee, I bet you could write a paper about me/us;" or, a nervous look and a sidle away as the person decides that I've been using my X-ray vision to see into them and their deep, dark secrets.

At this point, I believe the only people who don't have these reactions are either narcissistic assholes who think their crap doesn't stink, or those rare people comfortable with their own level of screwed-upedness, who have accepted that they, and everyone else, are all just pulling themselves up by their own frayed bootlaces.

So most likely, your secret fantasies are no more twisted than the ones lurking in the recesses of those around you. The overwhelming majority of people, more than 90 percent, never share their sexual fantasies with anyone, much less their spouses, friends or therapists. So, to a great extent, we really have no idea how many people out there have some really bizarre, screwed-up fantasies and interests.

But, if we were betting, I would put good money on you being shocked by the things that reside in the minds and libidos of the people you know. The book *Who's Been Sleeping in Your Head*, by Brett Kahr, tells the story of a sweet little Jewish grandmother. This nice little old lady, whose parents died in concentration camps, could only orgasm if she fantasized that she was tied to a doctor's table while Nazi doctors abused and examined her. That's pretty wild and sad, but guess what? It's normal. And for her, it was a healthy part of her sexuality.

From watching the modern media dialogue about porn, you're probably concerned that your sexual fantasies will at some point take you over and drive you into doing something you know you shouldn't do. That those fantasies of being raped, or raping, or any of the other extreme types of material out there will stop being just a fantasy and become a terrible reality that you can't take back. Like most people, you've probably had thoughts of murder and violence cross your mind when you were upset. You may even have indulged daydreams of clubbing your boss across the head, mooning your coworkers, and walking out of your workplace (Oh is that just me? Sorry.) But, you've never done it, have you? Sexual fantasies, daydreams, and desires are no different from others.

I suspect if a person is very worried about their porn/fantasies being exposed, they might be watching videos that are either very fetishistic or contain some significant elements of real or simulated violence. Maybe things like the "Facial Abuse" sites that are very dark, exploring the angry, scary underbelly of sex. The infamous videos "Two Girls and a Cup" depicted extreme expressions of degradation, which challenged everyone's sensibilities. Disturbing fetish videos are available where women kill or crush animals, and some people in the United States have been arrested and prosecuted for making such videos. Many of these videos are deeply disturbing and scary, touching into the same dark aspects of humanity that torture porn movies like *The Human Centipede* explore. But this material isn't new.

A long, long time ago, the Marquis de Sade published books and stories exploring these same dark elements of sex, pain and degradation. There's nothing novel about these fantasies and videos that are being watched, except that now these videos

are easily and widely available. What does that mean? Does that "click-of-the mouse" availability change things? It doesn't appear to. What it does is offer these images to people who were already disposed to react to them.

In other words, if you are watching and liking these videos, there's something in you that they are connecting with. And that was already in you before you saw the videos. I've heard this from lots of people, where they just happened on a certain form of porn, and it was like finding a secret treasure they hadn't known they were looking for. "It was the best nut I've ever had, jerking off to that porn."

Sometimes that image or fantasy feels like a puzzle piece that matches up to a part of your sexuality. What does that mean about your sexuality? It means that your sexuality, like everybody else's, is a complex, changing, and powerful thing that you are still learning about. Take these experiences, these questions and fears you have about your sexuality, and use them to understand yourself, your choices, your needs and your secrets. Shame only drives these things underground, and doesn't help anyone move forward in life.

Porn and Sexual Crimes

Rates of sexual offending go down as people in a society have more access to pornography. This is research that has been replicated in the United States and around the world. People don't talk about this because they don't want to acknowledge what it means. **Porn is good for society. A society with more access to porn is a sexually safer society.**

Access to pornography may decrease rates of juvenile sex offending even more. If pornography were a moral-altering thing, turning weak-minded people into rapists and pedophiles, it would have a greater negative effect on teen boys. And it doesn't. Just the opposite. Gay men watch more porn than straight men. But rates of rape and sexual violence in gay men are lower than in heterosexuals.

Being able to masturbate to a fantasy actually reduces the chances that a man will act on the fantasy. This holds true even for the scariest fantasies, which include rape, violence toward or others or to animals, or even child sexual abuse. I don't endorse it and find the issue extremely disturbing, but the data are clear. Access to real, or even simulated, child pornography probably reduces the rates of actual child abuse.

The way I think about it is that many individuals may be disposed, whether by biology, psychology, or environment, to be sexually aggressive. But most of those individuals, if they have a legal alternative, will pursue a safer, legal, private option. If they can go to a sexworker, jerk off to porn, or incorporate that aggression as a part of their sex life with a consenting partner and get their rocks off that way, they WON'T rape.

Many people might not like that message. I've had many sex workers acknowledge this truth to me and view their work as a form of public service. Some have resented this and felt that it was too much to ask for them to "absorb" such potential in order to protect others, who usually shame and reject them. Despite these outlets, a small percentage of men will pursue rape and sexual violence because for them, it is about far more than just sex. It is about their fear, anger, and aggression. Right now we don't really know how to pick out which is which.

Before he went to the death chamber, serial killer Ted Bundy told minister and psychologist James Dobson that porn magazines had turned him evil and into a raging killer and rapist. In contrast, in the book *My Father, the Pornographer,* Chris Offutt describes that his dad, author of countless hardcore bondage and BDSM novels, often said that pornography had actually prevented him from becoming a serial killer and acting out the violent fantasies of sadism that lurked in the back of his mind.

We are told by media and society that men and women who rape or sexually abuse people are sick, disturbed and unfixable. They might as well be dead or castrated. Unfortunately, I've worked with these folks, and I can tell you that isolation, rejection, and shame just makes the problem worse. A lot of smart people now believe that things like pedophilia have a lot to do with biology. I know some men, who are pedophiles, attracted to children, who are trying desperately to be "virtuous" and to not hurt a child or act on their desires. I'm sad that these men have these struggles. I wish it could be easier for them, not least because I know that the harder we make it for them, the more likely they are to give up trying.

Behaviors like rape and child sex abuse have to do with lots and lots of things—from biology to poverty. Some men ARE disposed toward rape, whether because of their background, their genes, or things that have happened to them. Some of these men are angry and narcissistic, and view rape of women as acceptable. Some men abuse alcohol and drugs, which lowers their impulse control and judgment. If these men watch violent pornography, it DOES increase the chances they'll engage in rape. ***These men probably shouldn't watch violent pornography, and I hope that they get the help they need and never rape or hurt another person.***

But, MOST men are not disposed to become rapists. Even watching violent pornography will not change that. I believe that in our fear of the few people who engage in sexual crimes, we are ignoring the fact that the overwhelming majority of people want to respect the rights of others, want to engage in consent, and don't think rape is sexy. Let's pay more attention to that. Let's start to celebrate those people and how they do what they do, rather than let our decisions be driven by fear and reaction.

Watching Anime Porn Doesn't Make You a Pedophile

I remember years ago, treating an adolescent sex offender, whose porn of choice was cartoon porn involving Disney characters and the like. At the time, the treatment team was convinced that his preference for this porn was evidence of the deep rooted nature of his desire for sex with children. But was it? I look back now and realize that our clinical confidence was largely unfounded and based on faulty reasoning.

Anime, or animated/cartoon porn, in many different flavors is now available throughout the world. It's extremely popular in Japan, with things like tentacle porn and "bara" porn, which mostly involves gay males who are often portrayed as ogres, animals, or monsters. There's "yaoi" or "boy love" porn, which is anime mostly of underage males in gay relationships. Lots of anime depicts females as young, adolescent at best, in sexualized relationships with older males and older brothers.

Jessica Rabbit has been fabulously sexualized, as have superhero characters in comic books. Tijuana Bibles were comic book porn produced in the early 1900s, which used comic strips to present sexual storylines. Cuckold comics are a recent phenomenon, popular amongst fetishists, showing wives being fantastically unfaithful to their husbands in impossible ways. There's animated and cartoon porn that shows large women using their gigantic butts or boobs to smother skinny men. BDSM cartoons have been around for a long time, and you can even consider many of the erotic drawings and petro-porn from long ago to be the equivalent of modern anime porn, showing fantasy sex that isn't quite possible in the real world. Ultimately, that's what the anime porn really is. It's fantasy porn for people whose sexual fantasies can't be adequately expressed in the real world or live action porn.

It's easy and understandable for someone to look at anime porn and get concerned that the juvenile characters being sexualized could lead a viewer to begin seeing kids in a sexual way. But the majority of people interested in anime porn tends to be people who are heavily into geek culture, people who are into furry fantasies (furries are a subculture who dress up in animal costumes to express

aspects of their personality and identity), or those with other types of fantasies which are easier to depict in cartoons and drawings. They are watching for those elements, not the juvenile sexuality.

Sexual abuse of children occurs for other complex sexual and social reasons, not because of cartoon porn. Let's fix those other issues—poverty, isolation, parental support and education, and parental drug addiction. If there's still sex abuse of children once we've cleared up those major factors, we should definitely tackle things like porn.

Liking these materials and having these fantasies isn't "sexually immature." That implies that there's a certain kind of sex that is "mature," or "right." We all know that this is code for "heterosexual, monogamous, vanilla sex." Because that's what is "mature" according to the people who want to tell you how to have sex.

"Rule 34" emerges from a 4Chan discussion about the nature of the Internet. Rule 34 says, if you can think of it, there's porn of it. All the varied diversity and complexity of human imagination is reflected on the Internet, including every possible sexual combination, no matter how bizarre. Porn of a man in a Mr. Peanut costume getting oral sex from a woman? Yup. Porn of a naked spider woman that has sex with a man, then eats him? Yup. Tetris porn? Yup. Porn about Rule 34 itself? Yup. Lots of such porn is in the form of cartoons or drawings, depicting things that only exist in people's heads. Many of these porns involve sexualizing characters from fiction, like the hot gay relationships between Captain Kirk and Spock, or between Hermione Granger and Luna Lovegood. These things sometimes freak people out, because they involve characters from family or children's stories—but they're not about pedophilia, they're about an expression of a person's internal sexual imagination, wanting to explore the sexuality of these characters they love.

Sigmund Freud famously described what he called "the polymorphous perversity" of human sexuality and the ability to find sexual gratification from a wide variety of actions, body parts, images, and fantasies. Rule 34 is the demonstration that humans are deeply and complexly varied in our sexuality. The diversity of porn on the Internet is a demonstration of that magical, wonderful, sometimes disturbing level of variations. Nothing more, nothing less. That diversity is not evidence of immaturity. If anything, it may be a demonstration of our sexual creativity.

Now, all that said—are these kinds of comics and cartoons appropriate for kids who don't have the maturity to understand that what they are looking at is fantasy? Probably not. Just like any other form of media. That's why kids shouldn't be allowed to watch the movie *Jackass* until they're at least thirty-five years old. . . .

Porn X-Rays: What the Porn You Watch Reveals about You

Here's a secret—nobody really knows whether your sexual fantasies mean ANYTHING about you, the person you are, your personality, or your sexuality.

Years ago, one of my clinical supervisors told me that within a few sessions of therapy, I should know what a patient fantasized about while masturbating. It took me a long time to finally figure out that he wasn't telling me I should ask people what they envisioned while "clicking their mouse," but that I should be able to formulate an idea of what would stimulate that person based upon my understanding of their psyche. I should be able to intuit, for instance, that this person got off from thinking of being raped, of having sex while watched by others, of having sex with many other people, or maybe just with that one forbidden person.

I've seen some truth of this. For instance, one young man I treated loved to watch porn that involved humiliation and physical abuse of women. He watched the "Facial Abuse" videos of women being slapped, subjugated, laughed at, and treated in cruel, dismissive ways. As he and I worked together, we found that he had lots of anger toward women, pent-up rage about the many times he had been let down by the mother and older sisters who raised him. His feelings of betrayal and powerlessness were stimulated by these videos, and they resonated with something inside him. As we worked on these issues, and as he developed and experienced what he wanted—a caring, healthy, sexual relationship with a girlfriend—his interest in those videos went away. I never told him to stop watching them. But as his ability to care for women increased, his interest in what was shown in those videos went away, until finally, he told me one day that watching those videos made him feel bad for the women involved.

Understanding a person through understanding their sexual desires works. Sometimes. And sometimes not. But it's mostly an unprovable, untestable theory. It's based on an assumption that who you are, and your sexual desires, are fixed, unchanging things. They are, and they're not. By and large, people have pretty limited sexual interests. They find things that turn them on, and that work, and they stay with those things in fantasy and porn. A brain researcher friend of mine believes that most kinks are things that people encounter, which just happen to match their brain make-up and make it easier for them to orgasm. That kinky image or experience just happens to kick you over the edge of orgasm more easily, not because of addiction, but just because it happens to puzzle-piece match the way your individual brain was made.

Scientists Gaddam and Ogas examined the Google searches

of thousands of people and found that overwhelmingly, they have fixed, unchanging sexual interests and search for porn of the same type, over and over again. Sex and porn DON'T create a slippery slope, coated in sex lube, which leads people to seek out more and more perverse porn as they get bored with more mundane images. Instead, people, especially men, get pretty stuck on a few, restricted types of images, scenes, and fantasies.

How do they get stuck? Damn if I know, but the data are pretty clear that males do, far more than females. In one study years ago, scientists took baby sheep and baby goats (lambs and kids, yes, I know, calling them baby sheep and baby goats is pretty silly. Fuck off, leave my grammar alone.) and switched them. The sheep grew up with the goats, and the goats were raised with the sheep. After about two years, and after both males and females of each animal had reached sexual maturity, they switched them back, putting them with their original species. The females of both sheep and goats were able to adapt and successfully mated with the males of their own species, where they had previously mated with the males of the other species.

But the males couldn't do it. The male goats had developed a sexual preference for female sheep, and the male sheep had a fetish for the female goats. When presented with the females of their own species, they just weren't interested. For some reason, biologically male sexuality is more likely to get "stuck," and this is why fetishes like shoes, feet, exhibitionism, voyeurism, BDSM, and others are overwhelmingly male issues. Few, if any, fetishes are diagnosed in females.

We really don't know why fantasies or sexual arousal get stuck. People sometimes tell stories that getting spanked as a child when they are first beginning to experience sexual arousal is the cause of interests in BDSM. It's a nice story, sometimes on the money, but it's just as often untrue. Ultimately these are just stories and nice, comforting explanations for things that are very complex with many, many different causes, from biology and psychology to environment and experience. Maybe in a thousand years we'll explain it, but I doubt it. People are pretty damn complicated, and sex even more so.

So, did the porn and fantasies you are worried about get stuck like this? Maybe. Do they reflect something about you and who you are, or are they just an example of the accidents of fate and biology that happen in our lives, minds and bodies? Probably both. Can you do something about them? Should you?

Maybe. The young man I mentioned earlier, who watched videos of women being sexually humiliated found that these videos were less appealing as he became more aware of his feelings of anger toward the women in his life. The kid didn't magically turn into a sensitive New Age male, but he did learn to direct his sadness and anger toward specific people, rather than toward all women. He grew to accept that the hard things he had experienced were things that happened, but he could choose how much they affected his life and choices today. His fantasies were a symptom of his internal struggles. That young man had been rejected by multiple therapists, before he came to me, because his fantasies were so scary.

Over the past few decades, we've learned that people—men and women—have lots of fantasies and sexual desires that they keep secret for fear of judgment and social rejection. There is no certain link between a person's fantasies and their actual choices in life. The things a person fantasizes about don't truly say anything about what, or who, that person is, or what he will do in his life.

This point is really, really important, so I'm going to repeat it. Read it verryyyy slooowwwllllyyyy so it sinks in.

Sexual fantasies don't actually change people's behaviors.

Think about this. The most commonly reported male sexual fantasy is to have a threesome with two women, a desire endorsed by 70-90 percent of men. This fantasy is so common among men that it's treated as ubiquitous and perfectly normal for men to fantasize about. But few men actually ever have such an experience. **Less than five percent of men ever have a threesome with two women.** If sexual fan-

tasy actually influenced behavior and drove people to pursue making fantasy real (in men, believed to have less impulse control over fantasies), these numbers of fantasy and behavior would be much closer together.

Your fantasies and porn interests might tell you something about who and how you are. And they might not. But, they don't control you, and they don't define you. Look at these things as more pieces of information that you get to gather as you come to understand yourself. Can you change them? Should you? That's up to you. But make those decisions from a place of self-knowledge rather than letting other people tell you that you need to change because they don't like what they see in you, or don't like what they fear those fantasies might lead you to do.

Dealing with Porn-Related Problems

It's overwhelmingly men who experience problems, conflicts, and legal consequences for their porn use. One reason is simply that men use more porn. But, society at large fears male sexuality more, and especially fears the darker, more violent sides of male sexual fantasies. Beyond that, men experience problems around porn use, because men use porn and sex as a way to cope with negative feelings. Sadly, men receive little support or education around dealing with negative feelings, and in that loneliness and isolation, we can sometimes overuse a strategy that feels good. For all these reasons and more, men run into conflicts and problems around their porn use. Research and writing in this area has been stunted by decades of blaming porn, as opposed to exploring what the real conflicts and issues are. This section is just a start, sadly. As porn, technology, sex, and society constantly change, new fears, conflicts, and problems will arise. Not because of porn, but because of us. New solutions are needed, but they need to come from the same place of understanding behind these strategies. Behavior change is always easier, when shame and fear are removed from the issue.

Reducing Your Porn Use (When You Really Feel Like You Need To)

I recognize that there are times in life when men feel they are watching "too much porn," whatever "too much" is for them. Often, this happens when the men are overusing porn as a coping method. Typically, when I see these men, they've stopped doing things like exercise, self-care, talking about their feelings and stresses. They start to feel as though they are losing control to porn and that they simply cannot stop.

It's really hard to try and stop doing something, especially something that feels good, that you've done for a long time. It's easier to start doing something than it is to stop. Maybe that feels strange, but it's human.

As a young therapist, I was trained to tell people to imagine a giant red stop sign in their heads, and to scream "STOP!" at the top of their lungs, inside their mind. This was supposed to be a way of interrupting things like thoughts of using drugs, fantasies, or urges around sexual offending.

Here's the thing, this stop sign screaming strategy didn't work. In fact, it made things worse. It gave energy to these thoughts. It actually made these thoughts, desires, and fantasies more powerful. So, if you read the above paragraph and thought, "I'll try that," please don't.

By trying to stop using porn and failing, you might be making your problem worse. When you give up porn and masturbation cold turkey, and then relent a few weeks later, you're putting yourself on a "variable interval reinforcement" schedule, which is a very deep-rooted form of learning.

Instead of trying to stop porn cold turkey, try one of these strategies, and focus your attention on the things you want to be doing, instead of watching porn:

- Try to cut down to moderate use by:

  Setting rules for yourself—like, I can only look at porn if the moon is in the sky, or only on odd-numbered days of the week.

  Tracking your porn use. Dust off those old math skills and create a bar chart that shows your amount of use. Track it every day/week. Work to reduce the average across a week at a time rather than cutting it off entirely. Download a behavior-tracking app. Use an exercise chart. Do something that forces you to pay attention to what you are doing, when you're doing it, and how you're doing it.

- Reward yourself with something if you achieve a goal.
- Instead of focusing so much on porn and not using it, try to increase the amount of other stuff you're doing. In other words, rather than fighting against porn, fill your time up with other things and other activities. Give energy and attention to the things you want more of in your life.
- You might even use porn as a reward for yourself—only allowing yourself to watch porn when you have exercised that day or had a successful day at work.

It's important to figure out what porn is doing for you. You can't find other things in your life to take the place of porn if you haven't done an inventory of why porn is important to you and what its function is. Here are some starter questions for you:

- Is porn a diversion from boredom, offering sexual satisfaction or sexual adventure?
- Looking at your porn use chart, can you see any patterns? Are you using more porn after stressful days at school or work? Using more porn when you feel sad being home alone on a Friday night?
- Is porn a distraction from other things you don't want to do?
- Could porn be a distraction from things you don't want to think about?
- Is porn a way of getting some kind of sex that doesn't really exist or isn't available in your life?
- Is porn a way for you to relieve stress?

Now, take the answers to those questions and for each of them, figure out five things you can do to get that same effect instead of porn.

Then try to increase the frequency with which you do those things. You could even use watching porn as a reward for doing them. Like saying to yourself, okay, I can only watch porn if I get an A on this test. Or if I finally go to a gay bar, or an LGBTQ center, and talk to somebody else about what it's like being sexual. Or if I tell my girlfriend that I'm not really in love with her anymore and that we need to break up.

The point is, the power is not in the porn, but in you. Where are you going to put that energy?

The Guy Who Can't Stop Watching Porn

Since I started writing and talking about porn, I've heard stories about that guy. You know, the one who is masturbating to porn for hours and hours a day. He does it when he wakes up. Does it for hours when he gets home. Does it in the bathroom at work looking at his phone. Ends up in the hospital for creating sores and wounds on his dick.

These are the rare stories that make all of us question whether masturbation and porn actually COULD be an addictive illness. Now, lots of men will tell you that they remember periods in their life when they've chafed themselves raw, masturbating. Some men have taken this to a painful extreme, serious enough for medical treatment.

As far as I can tell, these stories are real, but extremely rare. They reflect a tiny percentage of the majority of people who masturbate, the many people who use porn, and the few people who experience problems from their porn use.

In every case I've seen, in real life and in case descrip-

tions, there's evidence that there are other things going on. This hypersexual masturbation and porn use is sensational and attention-getting, but it isn't the whole picture.

In some cases, there is something biological going on in the person's body or brain. This includes the effects of brain injury and such things as the effect of some medications for treatment of Parkinsonian conditions.

In most cases though, the frantic and seemingly uncontrollable masturbation may be a response to life changes, such as divorce or losing a job. Sometimes guys get fired from their jobs or have their wives leave them over such behavior. I always ask these guys if they can acknowledge that at some level, they wanted to get fired and wanted their wife to leave, but they couldn't do or say that for themselves. In other words, the porn apocalypse is sometimes self-sabotage on a grand and messy scale.

So, if you are that guy, what happened before you started on this porn binge? You can say "nothing," but in my experience, that's almost always untrue. There's always something. And the porn use is a distraction from it, a way to fix it, to ignore it, or sometimes a way to pour gasoline on a fire.

Figure out what the porn is doing, what its function is in your life, and you'll be headed down the road toward having more control of it.

Usually these are short episodes, which are inherently self-limiting. If you aren't working, you can't usually afford the Internet access and the computer or phone to watch porn, and eventually, this binge comes to a screeching halt. **I work with lots of homeless individuals and guess what—I've never met a single one who says "I lost my house and my life because of porn."** But, I have met many who say that they lost their house because they couldn't pay medical bills.

But in fairness, it may be a situation where you DO need to manage this behavior. So, find a way to manage or reduce your use, on your own, or chances are good that life will intervene and stop it for you.

When a man tells me, "I can't stop!" I tell him that it sounds more like he doesn't want to. If he wanted to stop he'd see that he could stop by giving away his computer, giving up Internet access, throwing his phone away, or going camping for a year. None of that will fix the real problems, but as long as you're focused on the porn, I'm of the opinion that you're not really that interested in dealing with the actual issues here.

There have been NO studies that examined the long-term outcomes of such behaviors. But I believe that in most cases, such periods of behavior self-correct. Sex addiction therapists baldly state, "Porn addicts can't get better on their own." Such therapists want your business and want you to believe you need them. They also say, "Porn is like alcohol." And you know what? Seventy percent of alcoholics get better on their own, without treatment. So if porn were like alcohol, the same thing would likely be true. Focus on life, instead of porn, and the porn problems will get better.

Managing Unwelcome Sexual Thoughts

If you watch lots of porn, and are finding yourself having sexual thoughts more often, more frequently looking at other people and thinking about sex with them, it's probably because you are increasing your sexual drive. Any sexual behavior, whether it's masturbation or intercourse, is like an exercise for our sexual muscles (and not just the physical ones). The more sex you have, the more your body wants to have sex, and the more sexual capacity it has. The more frequently you masturbate, the greater the levels of sexual hormones in your body, including testosterone, which then increase your level of sexual desire.

The fact that you're finding yourself looking at people around you and wondering what they'd look like naked, what they'd be like to have sex with, is a reflection of your libido and sexual desire. It's not that you have been "pornified."

Having sexual thoughts doesn't mean you must act on them. Sexual desires aren't demonic forces that make us do things against our will.

If you're uncomfortable with the degree to which you are sexually aware and responding during the day, or if you're distressed that you are checking out your co-worker, pay attention to this feeling. Pay attention to your thoughts and behaviors.

You can tell yourself when it is time to be sexual. If you

find yourself thinking sexually at a time when you feel it's not appropriate, try telling yourself, "Hey, I'll think about that later. Now it's time to focus on _____." It's important not to make a big deal about this with yourself. If you freak out, scream at yourself, or feel angry or frightened, you'll make the problem worse, by giving it energy. The best strategy is to calmly and matter-of-factly remind yourself that this isn't time for sex and think about something else, preferably the matter at hand. Instead of fighting your sexual thoughts and feelings, try to focus on other thoughts and feelings.

This takes practice. Don't expect it to happen all at once. Sometimes, even when you've gotten good at it, sexual thoughts might still surprise you. It's okay for you to be a sexual being. It's okay for you to have sexual thoughts, to be sexually attracted to people, and to think about having sex with people you wouldn't ever really have sex with. Even when you get turned on, you are capable of making healthy, responsible decisions.

Oh, and by the way—stopping porn use, masturbation, sex-

ual fantasy, etc., might have an impact on your sexual thoughts, or it might not. Yes, if you stop "exercising" those sexual "muscles," you might over time reduce your sexual energy. But, you might also make yourself less prepared to manage and understand sexual feelings when they happen spontaneously, which they do. It's like abstinence-only sex education—it doesn't stop kids from having sex. But it does increase the chances that when they do, they are less prepared to make good decisions about it.

Cutting porn out of your life might reduce your overall sexual desire, but it might not, depending upon your biological predisposition towards sexual arousal. But it definitely won't stop you from having sudden sexual thoughts about that person next to you in the elevator, in the doctor's office, or wherever, because those thoughts and feelings are natural. Accepting, understanding, recognizing, "owning" and managing our sexual arousal is a far more effective means of self-control than burying our heads in the sand and trying to avoid ever having such feelings.

Porn Doesn't Break Your Dick/Erection

Some Internet gurus with absolutely no health, medical, mental health, sexual, or science qualifications are going around saying that porn has caused erectile dysfunction and that men masturbating with "softies" is proof that there's something wrong. Guys sometimes don't get a full erection when they attempt to be sexual. Sometimes their penis stays soft. These guys blame the issue on porn and go on the Internet and television saying, "Porn broke my dick!"

This is actually the way penises work. I'm sorry you didn't get an instruction manual issued with your penis. I didn't get one either. Urologist Dudley Danoff wrote a great book, called *Penis Power*, which is the closest thing I've ever seen to a penis instruction manual. (He doesn't say ANYTHING about porn causing E.D. by the way ...)

Look, you have to relax in order to get an erection. Sometimes, relaxing is really tough. Turning off your brain can be a hard thing. Sometimes, your penis doesn't want to get hard. Only worry about it if this is a constant thing, which keeps happening. Then, your doctor or urologist will ask you if you get hard while sleeping. If you do, then chances are pretty good that what you're experiencing is psychological.

That means it's tied to stress, anxiety, depression, guilt, or relationship issues. Maybe this is a problem. And maybe it's not.

By masturbating to porn, you've taught yourself that porn is arousing. You, your body and your dick, can learn to get hard without porn. It might take some time. But the learning process here is a part of normal sexual development and the ways our bodies learn, and our behaviors change.

When you masturbate to porn, you are often relaxing in a way that you might not, when you are with a partner. Especially if you are afraid of whether or not you will get an erection. When that fear is there, you start monitoring your dick, to see if it's getting hard. If it isn't, you start to panic, worrying that you won't, and what that will mean. I've heard of some men interrupting sex because they couldn't get hard, and running to look at porn to see if they could still get erect. When they did, they blamed porn for somehow causing erectile dysfunction. It's kind, I guess, that they didn't blame the woman they were with when it happened. Though I wonder what this woman thought of the man, who treated her so casually, running away to look at porn, and to test his penis—it seems fairly clear that the penis in this situation, is more important than the woman.

The fact that men can still have an orgasm and ejaculate without getting a full erection actually means their penis and sexuality ISN'T broken. Male sexuality is about a lot more than the hardness of a penis. When I see such men in therapy, I tell them "Welcome to the wonderful wide world of sex that doesn't revolve around your penis." I encourage them to explore using their hands, their tongues, their ears and noses and toes, and all the amazing parts of them. Spend time on exploring other kinds of erotic intimacy. Often, by not focusing so much on their penis, or even caring if it gets hard, they do. That's a lesson in and of itself.

Abstinence Won't "Reboot" Your Brain

In the world of porn addiction treatment, there's a theory that addicts must be abstinent, on average, for about 90 days in order to "reboot" their brains and let their brains "change back to normal levels of neurochemicals." The idea is that there's a "normal," healthy way that your brain works and that too much porn or too much sex alters your brain and brain chemistry.

This is pseudoscience. This is bullshit snake oil. This implies that "normal" sex doesn't change your brain chemistry, whatever "normal" is. This is bogus marketing crap being spewed to use "brain science" because brain science is hot. It ignores the realities of the ways our brains actually work.

Your brain is constantly changing. Things that you do a lot of, your brain changes to help you be more effective at. If you've been watching lots of porn, then yes, your brain has become better at watching and responding to the porn. If you stop watching porn and start doing other things, your brain will slowly start to change in these new directions. It's not "going back" to normal. There is no "normal," not really. "You can never step in the same river twice," a smart man said thousands of years ago. Your brain may change, but it's not going back to the way it once was. Not ever.

The other word for this changing brain process is "learning." Remember how it sometimes took a week or two after the end of school to get into different rhythms and relax into summer? Same thing here. You had learned to live and think and behave in certain patterns, and then you began unlearning those processes and learning new ones.

But, your brain is not a computer, which needs to be rebooted to clear out the RAM. If you think you need a break from porn, go for it. But don't go into it thinking that it is going to result in resetting your brain back to factory specs. Your brain will change again, learning in new directions and new patterns, based on what you fill your day with when you're not watching porn.

Instead of trying to reboot your brain, try learning some new software. Add some new behaviors, some new patterns to your repertoire. Enrich your life. Increase your RAM. We all know that rebooting your computer is usually just a temporary fix anyway. Time to start looking at a new computer, or at least making some changes in your life.

Loosen Up on That Death Grip, Bro

There IS a sexual dysfunction that is increasingly common in men who watch a lot of porn—delayed ejaculation. A common complaint from guys today is that they have a harder time coming during sex, especially oral sex, compared to when they are jerking off to porn. Dan Savage famously calls this the "death grip." Smart sex researchers have proven that Dan is right. The problem is that when masturbating, many guys are clenching their cocks tighter and harder, with more intense stimulation than another person's body can provide.

Essentially, guys are teaching their bodies how to respond to stimulation, and by using such intense squeezing, it can be difficult to orgasm once your body learns to expect that. Now, masturbation is great and a fabulous place to learn what sensations your body enjoys.

But, here's the thing. Guys can be really, really lazy. We find a certain pair of pants or shoes, or restaurant that we like, and we settle in. We like what we like and see no real need to change. Maybe calling it lazy isn't really fair. It's also about comfort and finding those things that feel good, help us to self-comfort, like a baby sucking on a tit, and seeing no need to change from what works. The same is true in masturbation and in porn. Most guys masturbate over and over in exactly the same way. They watch the same kind of porn 99 percent of the time. So, when it comes to jerking off, it's really easy for guys to stuck in a rut and not even know it.

Until they have sex with someone and find they can't orgasm without masturbation. Now, that might not really be a big problem—after all, many women need clitoral stimulation from their own fingers or a vibrator to orgasm during sex, and there's been a large campaign to normalize and accept that. But for men, there's still a very powerful message, both internal and external, that penis in vagina sex, or a blowjob, are the ultimate tops in sex. And if they can't orgasm from that, there's something wrong with them.

Maybe, but maybe not. When a guy is struggling to orgasm during sex, it can help him to understand all these different factors. But sometimes a guy does want to change this and be more able to be sexually responsive. It does feel good to be able to orgasm during that blowjob without having to take over with your hand. Sometimes though, this difficulty achieving orgasm has to do with being able to feel vulnerable, receive pleasure, or give up control during sex. But, the death grip is the first part of this to tackle.

So the first way to achieve this is to loosen up that grip while jerking off. Try using just one finger and your thumb. Try using your other hand. Try using just your fingertips. Try a

Fleshlight or another kind of sleeve toy made for penises, which provides wraparound sensation, but doesn't squeeze so hard. The first few times you try this, you might get frustrated. Like, really frustrated. Because it's going to take you a lot longer to orgasm. But don't give up. If you give up and squeeze your dick in that death grip, you're just keeping the problem.

It will take a few weeks, maybe even a month or two, to acclimate your body to new sensations and stimulation level. But you might find that the orgasms, and the sexual experience, are different in pretty amazing ways. Not more "right," just different. Different can be exciting and wonderful. Sometimes, when we're stressed, we just want that comfort, we want that comfort food, that soft comfortable hoodie, and that nice easy orgasm. It's your job to pay attention to your moods and needs, and be mindful about how to give yourself what you need and want. Easing up on the death grip is a good way to have options. . . .

Watching Porn Is Actually a Great Way to Relax (Too Great?)

There's a social belief that sex and porn shouldn't be used to relax. That sex shouldn't be a coping method, and that the very effectiveness of it could make it addictive. Why is it okay for people to use exercise as a way to cope with stress but not sex?

This is an area where many men and women differ. In general, men look at sex and porn more pragmatically, viewing it as a fun activity, as a way to cope with stress, as a distraction, and as an adventure. Women are more likely to view sex as either something that is for making babies, or developing a monogamous, permanent, emotional relationship. Not ALL women do this, but in general, more women see sex this way when compared to men. I'm not sure there's a right or wrong here, just a difference. Television does something similar. Kids often demonstrate something I call "TV head." They're watching television for a couple hours, and then when you turn it off and tell them to do homework or clean their room, they flip out, scream, cry, and bounce off the walls. This is related to what goes on in their brain as they watch television—when we watch television, the parts of our brain that self-regulate our emotions shut down, because they're not needed. Television tells us how to feel, with laugh-tracks and music and such. When the television goes off, that part of our brain is "down-regulated" and can't kick into gear quickly enough to help children control their emotional reactions.

Sex, porn, and masturbation are also very, very good at turning off some of our brain. Sex is SUPPOSED to work like this. Our bodies and minds are programmed and built to go into a special mode when we are engaged in what I call the Four F's. When we're Feeding, Fleeing, Fighting, and Having Sex (ok, really, when we're Fucking), the parts of our brain that worry about sadness, anxiety, loneliness, and all those other hard things,

turn off. If you're being chased by a man-eating tiger, it's not the time to worry about whether you said the right thing to your boss, whether your partner is cheating on you, or whether people like you. "Just get the fuck away from the tiger!" is what your body is screaming at you.

For years, people have looked at this issue the wrong way. There is research that has identified that people who are using more porn than others are people who are dealing with more stress, depression, and life problems. Some have looked at that and said, "A-Ha! See! Porn is bad for you. It causes stress and depression and life problems." But just because two things happen together doesn't mean that one is necessarily causing the other one. And sometimes, our biases can lead us to think that the wrong one is the cause. In this case, it turns out that these men actually started using more porn AFTER they felt miserable and stressed.

Over the past thirty years or so, since the 1980s and the AIDS crisis, (coincidence? I think not!) our society adopted more views of sexuality reflecting the idea that sex is something pure, beautiful, emotional, and inherently important. So, jerking off to porn as a way to deal with stress or sadness was automatically painted as something that was bad, weak, and detracted from the value of sex.

Porn as a coping method can work very well on a temporary level. For temporary problems, that's great. When you have a cold and your nose is plugged up with snot, taking a whiff of ammonia will clear your nose out. For a little bit. But the virus is still there, and the snot comes right back.

The problem is whether you're doing anything about the actual causes of your difficulty. Some problems are more permanent, built into our lives, and require more planning and long-range attention. Alcohol, porn, vacations, exercise, and other activities can give you a temporary relief from the mental issues involved in the things you're dealing with. But none of these strategies do anything to actually change the problem. Sometimes, getting a break from the problem, reducing the stress temporarily, can be enough to give you some perspective.

But if your life sucks in a way that is stressing you out, and pounding your meat to porn is the only thing you're doing about it, you could create a problem for yourself. Porn's not the problem though. You are. Do something about dealing with the problems in your life. If you can't alter the things in your life that are so stressful, whether it's work, relationship, sickness, or whatever, then you should probably consider expanding your repertoire of coping strategies. Add in exercise, therapy, skydiving, drinking, sleeping too much, and goofing off.

It's not the sex or porn that is the problem, but the over-reliance on a single coping method, whatever that coping method is. If collecting model trains is the only way that you manage stress in your life, then pretty soon, I can guarantee that your wife is going to be pissed off about all the money and time you spend on the damn things and the fact that the basement is so filled with your miniature world of trains that she can't even do the laundry. When I see people who have only a single coping strategy, I can almost always guarantee that the person is headed for a "train wreck," of one form or another. It's fine to have porn as one strategy. The important question is, "Besides porn, what ELSE are you doing to deal with your stress?"

When Porn Really Can Ruin Your Life

With the level of panic, fear, and legal concerns, you really need to be paying attention to issues porn raises. There truly are people suffering in jail, on sex offender registries, and who have lost their jobs, relationships, and worse, over porn. Acceptance, understanding, and peace with porn is still a long time down the road. While porn use is 99% innocuous and harmless, that 1% is something you need to think about and be aware of.

Porn at Work

Unfortunately, lots of people get fired for watching porn at work. This used to be a big problem. A few years ago, when the Internet was relatively new, and the Internet at work was faster than almost anything people had at home, there was a lot of porn watching happening at work. Some porn companies have reported that their busiest download days were the Mondays after long holiday weekends, when people went back to work and were looking at porn in the privacy of their office, away from their families.

But now, high-speed Internet at home is relatively cheap and accessible. Even more so, Internet and videos on the smartphone have offered people a much safer, more private way to look at porn, even when at work. People still get in trouble for this at work, usually because they're not thinking about what they're doing. A few years ago, one guy tried to sue a computer company he worked for, claiming that they created his porn problem by putting him on a computer with Internet access, where he was bored, just monitoring automated processes. He lost the lawsuit, by the way.

But bored at work is one of the most high-risk situations. Because you're sitting at your desk, trying to look busy, you start surfing the 'Net and clicking on interesting things. Like the Six Degrees of Kevin Bacon movie game, porn is never more than a few clicks away from any website.

Maybe it's not even hardcore porn. It's just nudes, stills from a Hollywood movie, celebrity leaked nudes. But it's a work computer, and in today's world of professional zero tolerance, it doesn't take much to be on the street with an embarrassing termination.

So, what do you do? Here's some tips:

- Come up with things to do if you get bored, stressed, or distracted at work. Take a walk, start writing your own book, take an Internet course on astrology. Before you're bored, not thinking, with half of your mind turned off, come up with things to do. Have a plan and then follow it.
- Turn your computer so that the screen is visible to anybody walking by your office. That heightened paranoia can be a healthy thing.
- If you are able to control your computer, put a monitoring/restricting program on it. Even if you keep the password to it, that momentary delay can slow you down enough to realize what you're doing.
- Use your smartphone to look up anything personal, whether it's porn or not. Don't use your work computer for personal email, shopping, or anything. Many employers are already monitoring their employees' computer use with software that stores any and all information. Do you really want your employer having your personal passwords?

- Schedule your porn use around your work schedule.
- Talk about your porn use with your wife to reduce your use of porn at work because you can't safely use it at home.
- Develop other ways to deal with stress or boredom at work.

In Brazil a few years ago, a woman was diagnosed as having hypersexuality and won the right to masturbate at work. She can literally close her office door and masturbate to porn on her work computer. It's like a woman's right to breastfeed at work. But there's not a hint that such a right could be earned in the United States or be awarded to men.

Let's acknowledge that there are tremendous hypocrisies here around porn at work. A person using porn at work might be a sign of sexual harassment or a sexually hostile workplace. But there's no evidence that this is always the case. We have to admit that things like Facebook or fantasy football actually waste a LOT more time at work. Unfortunately, none of these issues are likely to change, and it's up to us to manage around them.

How to Keep Your Porn Use Private

I'm not a computer guy, programmer or techie. So, to explore this issue, I went to the bench. What I got from a large group of tech-savvy folks is that complete computer privacy may simply be impossible. Methods of data recovery from computers are sophisticated and ever-evolving. So if you are looking for complete privacy, give up. Go live in a cave, masturbate to fantasies that live in your head, and never ever write them down. Anywhere. Certainly don't chisel the images into the cave wall—they last even longer than pictures on the Internet!

But, if you are looking some reasonable levels of control over your information and privacy, it is possible, so long as you

are willing to be diligent. The problem is when people get sloppy, lazy, or complacent and stop following these reasonable strategies.

Start with turning on the "Private" mode when you surf porn on your computer or phone. Most browsers, even on smartphones, now have this mode, meaning that information about what you look at on your computer, while in that private mode, won't be stored and easily accessible later. So it won't show up in your history or your cache. **But, Private Mode doesn't make you invisible. Information on what you looked at is still out there, on your ISP's (Internet Service Provider) records, in the records of the websites you went to, and to a degree, in your computer.**

You can go into your browser's settings and configure them such that the browser automatically clears the cache and deletes the history every time you close the program. If you want to keep naughty pictures or videos for yourself, you can use various applications and programs which create "hidden" files or locations for this material. Often, in order to access or even find these files, there's a requirement for another password. Don't make it the same as your other passwords. Choose something creative and unique. What's your favorite image to see in porn? "GodzillaBukakke" it is. . . .

Systems such as The Onion Router (TOR) offer anonymity online, bouncing your web browsing through secure, anonymous routers and making it very difficult to track back to you. While the NSA might be able to crack through some of TOR's anonymity, the average wife, boyfriend, or boss probably can't. But it looks suspicious as hell. Using it is a clear signal you are hiding something. Right? It's also clunky and can interfere in the ease with which you can navigate many sites. So you can use TOR, but you might get frustrated by slowness and glitches while looking at porn. You will be private. You might have to defend that you're not a terrorist or looking at child pornography and only use TOR because it's nobody's business what you do online. . . .

Finally, there are programs called cache shredders, which you can download and run. They go through the information stored in your computer's memory, essentially like a wood chipper. They make it hard to recover in any meaningful way, the information stored, even in hidden files.

But the world of computer information and data recovery is a constant battle. And frankly, the people who want to invade your privacy have a lot more money and power than the people who want to help you protect your personal confidentiality. When free, strong encryption technology became widely available, it was deemed a national security risk. Not because the government really wants to know what gets you off, but because they don't want to give up the chance to find that information out if they decide they DO want to know.

So rather than what is likely to be a fairly fruitless, frustrating and ever-changing endeavor, maybe you want to find other ways to assert your right to sexual privacy. What if you just said, "Hey, sometimes I jerk off to porn on this computer. What I jerk off to is my business. If you want to know, ask me and I may or may not tell you. But don't ask if you can't handle the truth."

How to Avoid Child Porn

Most men have zero interest in ever seeing child pornography. Less than zero. Watching or seeing child porn doesn't turn them on or turn them into a pedophile. But many men are terrified that by watching porn on the Internet, they might accidentally see porn involving kids.

Remember in *The Empire Strikes Back*, when Yoda says, "Yes, you should be afraid. . ."? Yeah. It's kinda like that. Because, while the absolute likelihood of accidentally seeing prosecutable child pornography is very low, the reality is that it does happen. Some people have gone to jail or have been placed on sex offender registries for accidentally downloading files that contained child porn.

Maybe these guys are lying, and they really were looking for kiddie porn. But all the indications are that in some rare cases, it was accidental. In today's reactionary and terrified/terrifying world, being accused of any sex crime, much less child porn, is like being sentenced to a torture chamber during the Spanish Inquisition. Once such allegations are made, a man's guilt is assumed. Allegations quickly become public and the media turn the screws, while everybody you've ever known watches.

But, here's the other, less scary side of the story—child pornography is usually very difficult to find. Much less than 1 percent of pornographic searches online are searching for child-related images—fewer than 2 out of a 1,000. The people who seek this out are intensely dedicated and focused on their specific interests, and they really have to work hard to find it. If you just jumped online and Googled "child porn" (Please don't, I beg you—doing so will literally put your name, or at least your IP address, on a list somewhere) images and videos are not going to just pop up the way they do if you search for, say "anal clown giggle sex." (Go ahead. I'll wait. Nice makeup they used, huh?)

In fact, many of the "easy to find" child porn sites are actually traps, set by law enforcement folks to catch those sad, clueless people dumb enough to think it's that easy. As an aside, from a Darwinian perspective, by catching all the dumb ones, aren't they actually creating smarter offenders who will get even harder to catch? Just saying.

Instead, most people who obtain child pornography do so through file-sharing activities, through online groups, in a maze of secret chatrooms and fake identities. They sometimes embed child pornography in other, seemingly innocuous files that are shared through services like Torrent or Limewire. They use programs like TOR to mask their identities and a dozen other ever-evolving strategies.

What you can encounter is porn with actors who look like they COULD be underage, and you might not be able to prove that they are. A British attorney told me about a client charged with child porn. The attorney was able to get child porn charges dismissed by tracking down the makers of the video and demonstrating to the court that the actors were in fact adults. He was only able to do this because the video was identifiable and could be tracked back to the producer. If you are watching pirated, stolen or even amateur porn, that option might not be possible.

You might also encounter images of nude children, such as at nudist camps, or the types of nude images that exist in antiquity and art. Here, you are in a grey zone. This material MIGHT be called child porn, or might not. Some legal cases have successfully defended artists with such material, of their own kids for instance, as protected and non-pornographic. But, Pee-wee Herman was forced to register as a sex offender, allegedly for having such images amidst a very broad collection of erotica and pornography. The very dangerous thing on the Internet right now is that anyone can put anything up there for everyone to

see. "User-generated material" is what drives sites like Tumblr, as well as porn aggregators such as the tube sites. Those sites aren't usually legally bound to screen material or verify their legality. If they find out something is illegal, they delete it, and may even then cooperate with authorities and share information about every IP address that ever downloaded it. However, many of these sites are operated by companies outside the US, who are not subject to many of our laws.

So how do you avoid that risk? You can definitely be safer from charges or accusations by paying the fee to view material by a reputable, established, regulated porn company. I do suggest joining sites that are in the same country or region as you—more chance they are under the same laws as you. Granted, then those charges are on your credit card bill, so there you go. Keeping your porn use secret is hard to do safely and liability-free. . . .

If you do search the free porn, think about what you're

looking for and the risks that might be embedded in that search. If you're looking for "teen" porn, yes, 99.9 percent of that is performers who are eighteen, nineteen and early twenties, who look younger. But if you accidentally run into child porn, how's that going to look when the investigators go through your history and find that's what you were always searching for? "Sure, buddy, you just found this accidentally. . . ." But if you're searching for MILF porn, or even GILF porn, maybe you've got more plausible deniability and even less risk of accidentally stumbling on any child porn or even questionably aged material.

Being mindful, conscious, and intentional about the porn you choose to watch is one of the most effective ways to avoid being accused of accessing illegal pornography.

What to Do If You Accidentally Download Child Porn

One thing that many men are surprisingly nervous about is what they should do if they accidentally see or download child porn. As I've talked about this book, and that question, I've been surprised at people's reactions. Most guys nod their heads and go, "Yeah, that's a real concern." Surprisingly, most women have expressed surprise at the question or concern. For some reason, most women, even those who use porn a lot, don't seem as worried about this. I guess it makes sense. Overwhelmingly, people charged with online sexual offenses for child porn are white males.

This is a concern mostly for men, and it is a legitimate concern. In one California case, a man used a file-sharing website to download a bootleg version of a Hollywood film. Unbeknownst to him, that file contained an embedded child porn clip and was being used like a "mule" to covertly share child porn with other people. When that computer file got tracked and identified by the law, they showed up at the guy's house months later. He had deleted the file when he found the child porn. But he didn't do anything else. And he's now on the sex offender registry, convicted of possessing child pornography.

If you accidentally see or download child porn, you'd probably be shitting your pants and thinking about setting your computer on fire. That seems like a perfectly normal and understandable response to me. But is it the right one? What should you do? Is it possible to be safe in that situation?

To answer this question, I actually interviewed several different attorneys and law enforcement officials. I also interviewed the surprisingly helpful and kind folks at the FBI. Let me tell you, I was more than a bit nervous in making that request. I'm sure the FBI said internally, "Yeah, this guy wants to know how people should deal with 'accidental' child porn. Let's run a search on him!" But, in fact, they were very supportive and understanding, and they agreed with the value of what I was writing. So I did the best I could to investigate this issue. I put my neck out on the line for you.

There is a very complex web of interconnecting law enforcement agencies around the world, who fight child pornography. Local law enforcement agencies like city and county police and sheriff's departments usually have some involvement, the FBI has a large department dedicated to this, and Interpol has a division that fights child pornography worldwide.

So, if you accidentally download child porn, you COULD delete the info from your computer, pull the hard drive out, beat it to death and set it on fire. But the fact is that your IP address, having downloaded that file is on record somewhere. And you can't delete that. And that large, vigilant group of law enforcement agents are out there, aggressively fighting to find and prosecute child porn and crimes against children. Chances are really good that if they don't know about it already, that file or picture you downloaded will probably come to their attention at some point. And then they'll work to track down everyone who ever downloaded it. Including you.

So, what should you do? The best, most ethical, safest, and smartest thing, is to call your local police department and report it to them. Be prepared to turn in your computer and don't expect to ever get it back. You can also report the material at www. cybertipline.com, or call 1-800-843-5678. Information submitted there will be reported to law enforcement.

You will likely face some hard questions about how you encountered this material and what you were doing looking for it. But, these questions are easier to answer than interrogation about why you hid the porn, deleted it, and tried to avoid any accountability for it.

Plus, by reporting the material, children may be better protected, and criminals who distribute child porn may get punished. That's a good thing.

There are scammers who created a spam and virus that pops up messages on your computer, saying that child pornography has been detected on your computer. The scam works various ways to get you to send money or open your computer to greater infection. The FBI recommends that in some limited cases, where such a scam, spam or virus is involved, you should wipe your hard drive and reinstall software. However, if there is any concern that you might actually have child porn on your computer, know that doing so might appear to be interfering with an investigation. So this is a place to be very transparent and careful. I wouldn't do this wipe and reinstall until after I had spoken with law enforcement.

Revenge Porn

Many people prefer porn made with and by their lovers. I've seen multiple men who tell me that their porn of choice are images and videos they've made with their wife or girlfriend. "It's someone I know and love," they say. "I know she's not faking." "I know she's turned on because I was there, or because I know her and what she sounds like." "More than that, I love her and seeing her turned on and happy, that's a far greater turn-on than watching a porn star I don't know."

In that you're not alone. But when a guy tells his ex that he destroyed the porn but didn't? And then he posts it online? That moves into douchebag territory. That's why there are now laws and public outcry over "revenge porn" websites, where people post such pics in efforts to humiliate, shame and expose former lovers.

The ONLY ethical way to handle this is to ask a lover permission to keep the materials for your private use, even after you break up or end a relationship. They have to trust you enough to believe that you can have the materials and never put them on a revenge porn website or share them with other people. If you've already lied to your ex about the porn, you've screwed any chances of them trusting you. Burn those images into your brain and destroy them.

If you're thinking about putting that porn online, think twice. Think three times, please. Guys put homemade porn up on the web for a variety of reasons. This isn't a simplistic, easy issue, though people would like it to be. The reasons why men post such material online are complex, filled with individual nuance and based on context. We really DO have to understand and acknowledge these reasons in order to address this problem effectively in ourselves and in other men.

Here are some of the reasons why men choose to post such revenge porn online:

- To show off what a stud the guy is, that he not only got this hot girl to have sex, but she let him film it.
- To get revenge on the girl for breaking up with him and for hurting his feelings. Rather than admitting he has feelings and dealing with them, he lashes out and tries to take her down a peg.
- To be one of the "cool guys" that post such porn. There's a lot of peer pressure in those kinds of online communities. They want to be cool, and they want to share their porn with other guys—guys who have shared their porn with them.
- Because the guy is an idiot and doesn't understand how small the world has gotten and how easy it is for such material to get identified.
- Because the guy is "angry at all women," and he wants to "take women down off their pedestals." I think this is rarer, but it certainly seems present in some of the highest profile revenge porn cases.

Which one of these reasons explains why you would be tempted to post that porn online? Do any of them feel like you? If so, you need to think about that, understand yourself, and do something about it. Deal with those feelings in other ways, not by breaking a person's trust.

Look, when guys post revenge porn, they're fucking it up for all the rest of us. Because now, when you're a guy who can be trusted with such pictures, it's harder for a woman to take the risk with you. Because they've seen all the dirtbag guys out there playing these games.

You CAN be ethical and responsible and make hot, sexy porn with your lady. But keep it to yourself unless you have her permission to share it. One clever strategy might be to offer her control of images that put you in a really embarrassing light. Like naked with a giant eggplant between your butt cheeks. It's the porn equivalent of the nuclear detente between the Soviets and the US. If you post your images online, she posts hers, and you both go down together.

Bareback Porn and Risk for Getting HIV

There's an intensely politicized debate raging about whether porn performers should be required to use condoms in sex involving any males. Much of this debate began in the 1980s in response to the AIDS crisis, and fears that unsafe sex could be promoted or encouraged by condomless porn.

Concerns over STIs in porn have led to draconian rules in porn made in the United States. Performers are required to have frequent testing, at their own expense. But these rules have largely worked. There are very few instances of on-set infections. Those that have occurred are sad, unfortunate tragedies. But for an industry that revolves around lots and lots of sex, that's pretty impressive.

But an important question in this debate is whether watching condomless bareback porn impacts a person's ACTUAL sexual behavior. If you are into watching lots of porn sex without condoms, does that mean when you get the chance to have actual sex with another person, you are less likely to use a condom?

There's no clear answer, mostly because this is a complex situation and the decision to use condoms is impacted by a lot more than the porn you watch. You might like bareback porn BECAUSE you like bareback sex—so which came first, the chicken or the (condom-covered) egg? In many people, the role of drugs and alcohol has a lot more impact on whether a person chooses to use, or demands that you use, a condom.

Further, if you can "scratch that itch" for risky bareback sex by masturbating watching bareback porn, it very well might reduce your urge to jump on Craigslist or Grindr and find someone for anonymous unprotected sex. Many gay men have reported just this, sharing that masturbation to arousing porn often helped them to avoid going out and having unsafe sex. The existence of satisfying, arousing bareback porn might be a release valve, reducing unsafe sex.

These questions are important for gay, straight, bi, and all others out there. When the AIDS crisis started, bisexual men were demonized for spreading AIDS. Turns out, it was mostly untrue and just more fearmongering. It turns out that gays, bisexuals, and people in open relationships are MORE likely to use condoms and practice safe sex, as compared to straight college students or heterosexual cheating spouses.

Now, all of these questions are really prompted by the fear of HIV. Because HIV and AIDS were demonized as a death sentence, and condoms or abstinence were the best protection, this is how and why condoms got inserted (ahem) into this debate. Nobody seems all that worried about protecting porn performers from other STIs. In fact, the chances of getting an STI on a porn site are far lower than the risk you hold if you pick up a person at a bar. But the fear that is embedded in the idea of HIV/AIDS is a powerful way to manipulate people's opinions.

But the question about HIV has changed, though you might not know it. First, medical research shows that current treatments are very effective at reducing the viral load of HIV, to the point that it is usually not trans-

mitted, even during unprotected sex. Secondly, the medication known as Truvada, or PrEP (Pre-Exposure Prophylaxis), appears to effectively prevent the transmission of HIV. Taken regularly, or even just taken a few hours or a day before unsafe sex (and for a day or two after), this medication reduces HIV infections dramatically. In multiple studies of it, there have been no transmissions, even in couples not using condoms, where one partner is HIV+ and the other is not. A single incident of HIV transmission may have been identified, which appears to relate to a relatively rare strain of HIV not affected by the medication.

But Truvada and this prevention strategy hasn't taken off or gotten much attention. Why? Because, at their core, people would just really rather you be afraid of sex. They'd ultimately prefer you not have that sex that they don't like. Bizarrely, the foundation that opposes porn without condoms has also resisted and opposed people using Truvada.

Some gay male porn stars are strong advocates for each other taking PrEP as a means of reducing the risk of HIV in their industry and in society at large. Others are afraid that they could be forced to take the medication, in a requirement that exists in no other professions. Like any other medicine out there, Truvada has side effects and risks. It's not a magic pill, and no one should think so. It's not a vaccine and doesn't prevent other sexually transmitted infections. But for the first time, it offers options regarding HIV and a way to respond to the fear, panic, and stigma around HIV.

> For years, we've made [HIV-positive] guys the ones responsible for safe sex, and if a transmission happens, it's their fault. That mentality has been a harsh but un-avoidable burden on poz people, and is the reason many still choose to only date other poz people. With PrEP, an

HIV-negative person can now more equally share the responsibility. Going forward, PrEP will make it so that we
are all responsible for preventing HIV, and as more people
get on the drug, we will all be helping end it.—Eric Paul
Leue, Executive Director of the Free Speech Coalition

So now, ethical porn doesn't necessarily require condoms
for prevention of HIV. You can feel better watching that bareback porn if those performers have the opportunity to be on
PrEP and protected from HIV transmission. Alternatively, you
can feel good knowing that the performers were offered the
right to ask for condoms to be used, as is now the practice in
multiple ethical porn companies.

The goal here is for performers—male, female, trans, and
everyone—to have the opportunity, information and right to
make the best decisions for themselves about their behaviors and
the risks associated with those behaviors.

But if YOU are a person who likes bareback porn, and you
have unprotected sex in situations where you don't know the
HIV status of your partner, you should do the same damn thing.
More important than stopping watching bareback porn is what
you do in real life to minimize your risk and contribute to a
safer world. Take responsibility for your behavior and your own
risk. Talk to your doctor about whether PrEP and other means
can prevent and minimize your risk. That's the smart, safe, and
ethical thing to do if you are going to engage in high risk sexual
activities. If you don't do that—don't blame porn.

Watching Porn Safely

It is possible to watch porn safely and to take steps to avoid getting in trouble for your porn use, whether that trouble is from

wife or girlfriend, or from the law. A more interesting question is, "How can I continue to watch porn responsibly and not fear that I will be seen as a pervert for doing so?"

The ever-brilliant Dr. Marty Klein says that the problem with the laws on porn and sex is that when such laws are enacted, everyone pretends they are lily white virgins who've never looked at porn or even thought about having kinky sex. So we don't protest such laws, for fear of being painted as immoral and perverts, simply for protesting.

What it takes for you to be safe, for me to be safe, for your friends and my friends to be safe, is for there to be greater social recognition that men can, and do, watch pornography responsibly and safely.

It requires you, and other men and women who use porn as a healthy part of their sex lives, to stop treating porn use as a dirty little secret. It's private information. But even private information, like your medical history, is something that we are comfortable sharing when and where it's socially important and appropriate. As Klein has said, if there were laws prohibiting prostate cancer treatment, you'd stand up and say, "That's not right. I had cancer treatment and it saved my life," even though you might not tell everyone you met that you had prostate cancer. Right?

You don't have to shout, "I watch porn!" from the rafters. But the next time you are part of a conversation that treats all porn the same, that spreads myth and Chicken Little fears about porn, you do need to try to say something like: I watch porn sometimes, and it hasn't turned me into a rapist or a child molester or a creep. I've learned something about myself from watching porn. The problem with porn is that we are not having the right conversations about it. It's not something that we should fear.

Guilt,

Religion,

and Porn

It turns out in recent research, that most atheists don't worry too much about their porn use, or feel all that guilty about it. A person's religious attitudes towards sex are a much better predictor of how they feel about their porn use compared to how much porn they actually consume. In other words, if you're feeling guilty and ashamed about your porn use, chances are really good that it has a lot to do with your religious and moral beliefs. The reality is that most of these values about sex were developed in very different times, in a very different world, when sex was simpler (not better, and really we only pretended it was simple and ignored evidence that it wasn't), and where guilt and shame were the most effective means at hand to control people's sexual behaviors. Like all outdated moral and religious rules, it's our job as adults to examine them and start to put them in perspective, in our lives and relationships, whether that relationship is with a sex partner, or with a higher being. Here's where you get to start figuring out what kind of sexual person you choose to be, and how you want to live your sexual life, as opposed to being told what sex acts not to do. Here's the scary part—right now, religious people are more concerned about porn than they are about gun violence or racism. So, putting these things in perspective is very difficult and scary, and requires looking at the world, yourself, and your morality, in a whole new way.

Porn-Related Guilt

Some people, both men and women, don't like porn because of the way it makes them feel. Not aroused, but sad and guilty.

Or more often, aroused and then guilty and scared afterward. They worry that many of the girls in porn are on drugs or doing porn just because they're broke, or they were abused as children. They worry that watching and sexually enjoying this porn is the equivalent of taking advantage of the women. It's easy to believe these things, and in a way, you're supposed to feel guilty about those things—that's what the people who say these things want. **Because they feel bad about porn, they think you should feel bad about it as well, and they just can't understand how you don't feel and think the same way they do.** All porn is not created equal. And all porn performers and actors are not the same as every other person who has sex on camera. Treating all porn and all porn actors as though they are the same is part of the problem. This is a big, complex, varied business, and there are lots of different types of approaches to porn and different types of people who are in the business.

Studies of American porn performers have found that they are not the stereotype of an abused, damaged blonde with fake boobs. Instead, most female porn performers are brunettes, and the women report having been abused about as much as any other women in our country, which is sadly, far too much. Most American porn performers tend to be sexually adventurous people, who got into porn, at least in part, because they like sex.

Many performers in porn are educated, thoughtful, and passionate people. I personally know at least three porn performers with doctorates in varied degrees, who have taught, lectured, written, and worked professionally. Some of these folks got degrees while working in porn. Others got degrees and then decided that the rat race was too much, and that porn offered them more freedom to experience themselves in sexuality and life.

Note that I'm talking here about American, professional porn. We know relatively little about the people who make amateur porn, and we know even less about people in porn from other countries, especially non-Western countries. The laws that require documentation of consent and age verification are very strictly enforced in America for professional pornography. But there's little enforcement of this in amateur porn, and with porn made outside the US, all bets are off. There have been some sad incidents even in the US with amateur porn submitted to sites, turning out to have been made by people involved in violent, coercive relationships.

One of the most recent insidious guilt-trip ploys is to blame porn for "sex-trafficking." In short, sex trafficking is when people are forced into sexwork against their will, often transported to other states or countries to work in sex. There are sad, tragic examples of this happening, particularly in other areas of the world, where poverty, war, and refugee status make women and children vulnerable. But, the role of sex-trafficking in porn from the Western world is practically nil. Most claims of sex trafficking in the US have turned out to be inflated, exaggerated and manufactured in order to prosecute sexworkers. Ethical, transparent, and legal porn is the best way to combat this risk, frankly. Sex trafficking is of greatest possibility in porn that is made underground, illegally and in secret.

Long story short, you're right to be concerned about this stuff, but there are ways that you can watch porn and not feel guilty about it. In other words, you really can find "fair-trade porn." You can search for things like "ethical porn," "feminist porn," and "indie porn," as ways to target porn made by people who are paying attention to these issues.

Our entertainment industry is based on exploitation, whether we are talking about football players with concussions, or Disney performers who spiral into drugs and self-destruction. I think more people need to be ethical and responsible about the entertainment practices and industry we support, in all of these entertainment areas, not just porn.

Ethical porn is out there. This is made by producers who pay their performers, who take no for an answer, who don't force their performers to have condomless sex if they don't want to, and who don't change things in the middle of a scene, but have communicated openly and effectively with their performers.

Why are you feeling guilty about your porn use? Before you can really move forward resolving this guilt, you need to figure out where it comes from and what feelings or beliefs make you feel so bad. Here's some starter questions to explore:

- Growing up, did people tell you that porn is wrong?
- Do people in your life tell you that porn is bad?
- Does your religion or religious leaders tell you that porn and masturbation are evil?
- Does the porn you watch connect to a secret in your life and sexuality?
- Are you feeling guilty about the porn, or is it the sexual desires you are ashamed of?
- Do you believe that you shouldn't need porn or masturbation in your life?
- Are you afraid of getting in trouble for porn? With whom and why?
- What would happen if you went public with the kind of porn you like?
- What do you think would be people's reaction if your porn browser history was public to all your Facebook friends?

Porn and Religious Morality

Porn is immoral, right? The Bible says so. Most religions condemn porn. Lots of people get turned on watching porn, but then feel absolutely miserable, guilty and ashamed of themselves afterward.

I'm not a priest, not a minister, not an arbiter of what is moral. So take everything I say here with a grain of salt.

I'm not opposed to religion. I think religion and Belief (capital B Belief) is incredibly important for many people, and for humanity in general. Like most things that are human, we found ways to fuck it up and use it make things hard for other people. That doesn't diminish the value of religion, it just means it's human and that we as a people are at least consistent. We will screw things up, no matter how well intended we are. But we always keep trying and keep hoping.

I'm not all that clear that the Bible speaks against pornography or masturbation. The Bible condemns lust, shamelessness, lascivious behaviors, immorality, and fornication in general. It's often believed to condemn masturbation, but the story of Onan, often understood as a prohibition against masturbation, is actually wrapped up in an ancient practice called levirate marriage. This story is about economics and inheritance rights, not about masturbation.

At least one significant historical and social function of religion was to exert control over reproduction. This control was necessary in a world without effective contraception. So, at least in part, many of the religious prohibitions that controlled sexual behavior are now out of date or at least only moderately relevant.

Sexual values built into religion were developed in different times, under different circumstances. They apply today, only as much as we choose to allow them to. We no longer stone people to death if they cheat on their wives or husbands.

Biblical prohibitions against marital infidelity and divorce are clear. But they haven't stopped the tide of infidelity, divorces and remarriages that sweep our society generation after generation. We now recognize that divorced people can still be moral. That a person who is sexually unfaithful can still have integrity in other places in their life. Why isn't the same true, for masturbation, pornography, or lustful persons in general?

This issue is, for me, one of the most important ones in this book. Much of the shame and secrecy around porn use is based on a deep-seated fear that it is inherently immoral, and unforgivable. I choose to reject that blanket, unrealistic, and irrelevant prohibition. I believe that a person CAN choose to use porn in a moral, responsible, conscious way. You get to choose. In today's world, you are empowered with choices, freedoms, and opportunities never before widely available like this. You may decide that porn, in any form, is unethical and not a part of your life. You may decide that the concerns about porn are overblown,

and exaggerated—no more significant than issues related to any form of entertainment—and you're just not going to worry about them. But the choice is yours. Make it for yourself, with your eyes open, and without other people making it for you, with no idea who and what you are or your life is.

The Religious Institute is a multi-faith consortium of over 4,500 pastors, ministers and clergy from around the world, who advocate for sexual health, education, and justice. In their Declaration on Sexual Morality, they call out the religious condemnation of sexuality: *"Sexuality is God's life-giving and life-fulfilling gift. We come from diverse religious communities to recognize sexuality as central to our humanity and as integral to our spirituality. We are speaking out against the pain, brokenness, oppression and loss of meaning that many experience about their sexuality."*

They go on to demand something pretty close to what I'm arguing for:

> Our culture needs a sexual ethic focused on personal relationships and social justice rather than particular sexual acts.

So from a religious and a moral stance, if you are concerned about your use of pornography, examine where that use stands in the context of who you are, how you treat others, and yourself. Don't single out pornography or one certain form of pornography as some overriding indicator of your religious state of being.

Resolving Conflict between Your Religion and Your Porn

Folks in Utah are really scared of pornography. Really, really scared of it. Some of this is because Utah consistently uses more porn than many other states. But more than the frequency of porn used, there is greater fear about the fact that this porn use might reflect underlying problems with the modern world of sexuality. We are still learning how these dynamics work. More religious people use less porn. But more religious states overall use more porn. This may reflect religious people using porn, and/or it involves nonreligious people in those states using more porn because of decreased access to sexual expression in the society. I suspect it's both.

Many religious and political leaders want people to be afraid of porn because they think that making people afraid of porn will prevent them using porn.

There have been multiple political resolutions introduced and passed in the Utah legislature condemning porn. They see porn as destructive, warping sexuality in teens, changing their brains, turning them into rapists, and destroying marriages.

The dominant religion in Utah is Mormonism, or the Church of Latter Day Saints. Mormons are one of the groups who struggle tremendously with sexuality issues, especially any sex that is non-heterosexual, nonmonogamous, or doesn't "make babies." As a very conservative religion, they view sexuality outside marriage, homosexuality, abortion, premarital sex, even contraception with great suspicion, if not outright hatred. Pornography, masturbation, promiscuity, homosexuality, and most forms of non-vanilla, non-hetero sex are condemned. Utah continues to enforce abstinence-only sex education in schools, and for a while, even made it a crime for teachers to tell students about condoms or birth control.

I have a number of friends and colleagues who make a good living providing sex therapy to Mormon couples. These couples get married and realize they know next to nothing about sex. They find that they like sex and would like to make it better, along with dealing with all the issues of erectile function, orgasmic compatibility, and sexual communication that other couples deal with.

Utah has more porn addiction treatment programs than any other state, and is more focused on the issue of porn than they are concerned about prescription drug problems, racism, pollution, or gun violence. The president of Brigham Young University starred in a bizarre public service video, called "Wounded on the Battlefield." The video told young college men that if they did nothing when they knew their friends were jerking off to porn, it was just like leaving brother soldiers to die alone on a battlefield. Fight The New Drug (FTND) is an advocacy group promoting the idea that "Porn Kills Love." They're based in Utah, and they provide porn education campaigns throughout schools in Utah and elsewhere, arguing that porn affects people's brains just like a drug, causing erectile dysfunction along with a host of other problems. Much of the leadership of FTND have Mormon backgrounds, and some were previously involved in the Church's battle against legalization of gay marriage. They recently pissed people off in San Francisco, by posting huge billboards around the Bay Area. No one has ever sufficiently explained why they chose to target the city of San Francisco specifically.

But it's not just the Mormon Church struggling with these issues, though they are the most vocal at this moment. The Catholic Church has a long history of suppressing porn, locking it up in the Vatican, and funding anti-porn crusades. Catholics made a famous anti-porn video in the 1960s, called *Pages of Death,* which laid the blame for rape and murder on the corrupting influences of pornographic magazines and "smutty" books. Conservative religious groups such as Focus on the Family and James Dobson long opposed pornography and were the leaders in getting *Playboy Magazine* taken off the shelves of 7-Eleven stores.

For decades, these moral groups have painted their battle

against porn as a public health issue. They firmly believe that porn is dangerous to society, sexuality and humanity. But they can't seem to tell whether they are upset over porn as a moral issue or as a health issue. I'm not sure they can tell, honestly. They look at the existence of porn and have a moral outrage and sense of disgust so strong that it overwhelms their reason. They view as flawed, any science or research that disagrees with their sense of wrongness about porn. They really do intend to save you from porn. Whether you like it or not.

But what about the people in those religions, who, like you, watch porn? How can they understand this fight? How can they resolve this conflict within themselves and within their sexuality? Can they stay in that religion and feel at peace as they watch porn?

One thing such men do is seek out the hardest, "non-porn" they can find. The more religious a person is, the less likely they are to watch porn. But, they are MORE likely to spend lots of time going through swimsuit and lingerie catalogs, and they get good at finding the naughtiest, but still "non-porn" material they can find. This is one way to resolve their desire for visual sexual material, and their moral issues with porn.

Many religious men seek out or encounter porn and then feel awful about it. Because they've been told to fear porn and to be ashamed of their sexuality, they beat themselves up over it. The more people fear porn, the greater the porn they watch influences their thoughts, feeling and behaviors. Often, they confess their problems with porn to their religious leaders and supporters. When they do, they are met with greater commands to give up porn and to fight the evil that it has put in their soul. They are ordered into treatment, where they are told that prayer, faith and confession will heal their souls and prevent them from needing or wanting porn. But unfortunately, if they never deal with the real sexual, gender, and relationship issues that are involved in their interest in porn, these men will never be successful at understanding themselves, their sexual needs, or their sexual choices.

In 2015, a compassionate opinion piece was published in the *Observer* by a Mormon man from Utah, named Paul Malan. Malan's article is radically different from the shaming, fear-mongering, guilt-tripping approaches that are common in religious discussions of porn and masturbation.

Called "The Naked People in Your iPod," Malan's article explores a conversation with his son about pornography, what it means, and how to resolve porn use versus religion's condemnation of it. It's a delightful article, and I hope that you will find it and read it if you are a religious person struggling with porn in yourself or others.

Malan makes some wonderful points that I'm going to briefly summarize:

- Fear of porn keeps people from talking about it or getting help understanding it.
- Sexual desire is like any other human desire—no better or worse.
- Conservative religions really, really suck at talking about, understanding, or dealing with porn because they are deeply afraid of it.
- Religious opponents to porn treat normal sexual arousal and porn as identical. They tell people that the problem is that they get "turned on" by porn, and it does bad things to them.
- Because people in these religions can't really talk about sex, nor get much education about sex, they get confused and condemn themselves for getting turned on. They end up fearing porn, sex, and their own feelings of sexual arousal.

- The way to deal with porn is to remember that it is fantasy, and that it means only what we let it mean.
- Porn isn't the enemy, and when religions teach people to fear it, they only isolate and shame their own people.
- Wisdom around porn comes from being mindful and self-aware about one's use. A religious person struggling with their porn use should spend time with the question of "why" they are using it. Rather than fighting porn, they should work to better understand themselves and what porn means, and does, for them.
- Then, a religious person can make a self-aware, authentic decision about their behavior within the context of who they are and how they feel about their religion.
- Thus, porn becomes "just another thing in the world" that we can deal with. The porn industry has problems, which we can choose to ignore or, if we want to, we can try to try to address them and make porn better.

Though Malan doesn't say this last bit, I do. I believe that one of the best ways to resolve the conflict between our religious and moral values with our desire for porn is to commit to choosing ethical porn that we can feel better about.

Rather than opposing porn overall and fighting a frankly hopeless battle, I wish religious leaders would say instead, "Porn SHOULD be better, more ethical, and more responsible." This would give their followers a way to deal with their porn use—a way other than fear, dirty secrets, and crippling shame.

Got Negative Attitudes toward Porn? Then Don't Watch It.

Interesting research has been done around casual sex and its effects, both positive and negative. Basically it boils down to, what

are your expectations and attitudes toward casual sex in general? If you think that having sex with people you're not in love with is negative, that people who have casual sex are slutty or gross, you will probably end up feeling shitty about yourself and other people if you have casual sex! If you don't think casual sex is a big deal and think it's a fine form of relationship adventure and sexual excitement, then casual sex is pretty unlikely to have any negative effect on you. The point here is that casual sex is different for different people, depending upon a lot of things, and to say simply that casual sex is bad or good is a gross oversimplification.

The same thing is almost certainly true of pornography. If you think pornography is damaging to females, gross, addictive, or damaging to your sexuality, or if you view masturbation itself as something that is inherently unhealthy and dangerous, you will almost certainly experience negative effects and problems from pornography if you choose to watch it.

The problem isn't necessarily the porn, nor is it even your moral or sexual attitudes. The problem lies in the conflict between these two things.

If your behavior, your choices, are consistent with your moral and sexual attitudes, there's no problem. But if you feel deeply that there's something wrong with porn, and then watch it, you're likely to experience problems. And you're probably going to do what a lot of people do—project those problems onto the porn and blame the porn for the problems. It's easier to do that, and it's human to externalize and place the blame outside yourself, rather than looking inside and seeing where the conflict lies within ourselves.

People who blame porn for their pain are trying to find ways to reconcile their behaviors, their sexual desires, and their moral attitudes. The more any of us can put those things all together so that they mesh well, the less likely we are to experience problems related to our feelings of guilt, distress, depression, anger, and sadness around our behaviors and sexual choices.

If you are afraid of pornography and reject the idea of pornography as healthy, you're probably a person who shouldn't watch it. But you have to remember that not everyone feels the same way you do and is thus not likely to experience the same negative effects as you. If you feel negatively about porn, but really want to watch it, you have to find a way to resolve that conflict. Either stop watching it, or figure out how to change your negative attitudes about it. Your choice.

Talking to Your Therapist about Porn

I conduct trainings around the country, teaching therapists how to address modern sexual issues in therapy. Until recently, most didn't see these issues. Most patients kept quiet about them. If they got in trouble for sex, they were referred to therapists who told them sex was an addiction. Sometime in the 1980s or so, therapists really stopped talking much about sex, or getting trained on it. I think therapists wanted to divorce themselves from Freud's obsession with sex, and wanted to be like real scientists and doctors. But now, as society's sexual values are changing, and as healthcare is changing, offering greater access to counseling, more therapists are hearing about sex and porn in their offices.

Chances are sadly very good that your therapist has received little to no training in sexuality, and none on pornography. Most therapy-training schools provide no sexuality training, and therapists aren't usually required to have any for licensure. That might be hard for you to believe—sex is kind of important after all, but unfortunately, most therapists assume that they don't really need much training in this area. More than half of all therapists never ask about their patients' sexual needs, use of pornography, or sex life at all. Chances are that your therapist is female. That's not a bad thing and only reflects the fact that the therapy field, like nursing and teaching, has become female dominated.

So what this means is that the beliefs your therapist has about pornography are most likely based upon her own personal experience, her attitudes toward porn as a woman, and what she sees in the general media. Most therapists don't read academic journals and don't go to trainings about porn or sex. They think they don't need the training, that it might be offensive to them, or they are afraid that going to the training might "out" them as liking sex or porn.

Maybe you will get lucky and go to a therapist who likes porn, or has even been in porn (I know several in fact, former *Girls Gone Wild* now quietly doing therapy). If you can find a therapist who advertises as LGBT-friendly, or is trained by the American Association of Sexuality Educators, Counselors and Therapists (AASECT), your chances are better that the therapist won't just kneejerk and tell you that porn is bad and makes you into a rapist.

Unfortunately, this often depends upon where you are. If you're in a more conservative or rural area, you need to expect that your therapist is likely to have a strong and mostly negative reaction to porn. If you're seeing a therapist who identifies as a religious or Christian counselor, chances are extremely good that they are going to instinctively pathologize your porn use.

Most reasonable, good, secular therapists are going to see that porn is a small part of your life and not spend too much time worrying about it. IF you can be clear about it with them. Unfortunately, if you've gotten in trouble at work or are fighting with your wife over your porn use, you have an uphill battle here.

This is why most people don't tell their therapists about porn use. First, it's usually not a problem. Secondly, they know the therapist might react negatively. Unfortunately, this means that most therapists will react negatively because they're not hearing about these issues and they don't have any framework in which to understand porn, aside from the porn panic that inundates our popular media.

In other words, they're ONLY hearing about or seeing porn when it's a problem. So, they think it's ALWAYS a problem. I regularly receive emails or calls from other therapists who tell me that they are appalled at my "casual" attitude toward pornography use because they see the divorces and damage that porn causes in people's lives. If you see one of these therapists—good luck, my friend. They are certain that porn is bad and unhealthy, and their certainty is their evidence for their beliefs. Yes, that's circular, but you can't tell them that.

You can tell the therapist to read this book, to read any of the books or articles that I list in the reference section, to check out my writing, or that of my colleagues listed in the resource section at the end of this book. Almost all of us have had the experiences of talking other therapists down, who are freaking out and concerned about a patient's porn use or sexuality.

But you have to be prepared to tell your therapist the same thing you would say to your wife: "Look, my use of porn is a healthy part of my sexuality. It's a place where I can relax, enjoy myself sexually, get some sexy entertainment and explore sex. It's something I'm not ashamed of and is something that fits into my idea of who I am and the kind of sexual person I want to be." Then, you can tell your therapist that you would like their help in figuring out how to deal with the shame, fear, and guilt that gets heaped on you for your porn use.

Therapists are good at helping people heal from shame and guilt. It might take work for you to find the right therapist and get them to see that porn use isn't a shameful thing, but I believe most therapists, when it's framed that way, will genuinely be able to help.

Children, Teens, and Porn

Porn is fantasy for adults. But, through the power of the Internet, children have access to it. Because we believe that restriction of information and censorship is more dangerous than the consequences of immature people gaining access to information they cannot deal with, there is currently no global, universal way to prevent children from accessing it. Maybe there will be one day, but I have no idea what it could look like, and how it would work, to still allow young people access to educational material, self-help information, and to gain an understanding of sexual diversity, but block access to porn. For now, we must deal with the world we have, and in that world, teens are watching porn. To deal with this, we need to understand what it means when teens see porn, and also what it doesn't mean. Since the dawn of time, teens have been obsessed with sex. Porn hasn't changed that.

Porn and Teenagers

I went on Katie Couric's talk show a few years ago, and had an awful experience. It was a deeply troubling and challenging situation. Couric didn't want to hear about science, and she didn't want to hear about research that shows that porn exposure has little real impact on teens. Instead, she wanted to promote the idea that common sense says that porn is bad for teens, and that we should listen to that fear. She and her guests argued that porn warps kids' brains, that porn causes erectile dysfunction in young men, and that parents everywhere should be very afraid of their kids watching porn.

This show was one of the worst media experiences I've had,

and many of my fellow writers and psychologists rallied around me. In lots of ways, the show demonstrated the ways the media is feeding porn panic. But it taps into the very real fear that exists in many parents around their children's exposure to porn, and taught me a lot about the conversation we're not having about porn. Look, if you're a parent of a teen, do you really think your teenage son is NOT watching porn? Your teen son is watching porn, and probably your daughter is too, though less often. Back in the day, we stole our dad's *Playboy*. Now it's on your teen's phone and computer, and in the emails and texts they share with friends. Girls send your son naked pics of themselves, and he has probably sent them dick pics.

I'm not making light of this. Neither I, nor anyone, really knows what this actually means for your son, your daughter, their generation, and for our society. It's unlikely to spell the end of the world. I doubt your son will turn into a porn zombie and eat brains. His chances of getting a girl pregnant or deciding he's gay? Probably unchanged. Your daughter's chances of becoming a porn star, stripper, or lawyer? Unchanged.

Porn exposure in kids doesn't have a life-altering, warping effect on children. In fact, research by a colleague in the Netherlands showed that exposure to pornography explained less than 1 percent of the variance in adolescents' behavior. This means that 99 percent of the reasons why these kids do the things they do have nothing to do with the fact that they view pornography. What does explain about their behavior? Things like violence, crime, sexual behaviors, or drug use are related to other, far more important things in life like poverty, mental health, education, and family environment.

So, rather than worrying about whether porn will warp your son's sexuality and brain, worry instead about his education, about him feeling loved, valued, and heard. That you care about him and his future. Talk to him about sex and about porn. Do you watch porn? Does he know that? Can you tell him what you like about porn and what you hate? Can you let him read this book and talk to him about it?

Politicians and religious zealots oppose teens learning "bad" sex from watching porn, but hypocritically also oppose sex education that would help the teens learn how to have good, responsible sex. They can't have it both ways.

Our society is going to spend the next generation or two dealing with the aftermath and lingering effects of abstinence-only education. Even though it's no longer federally mandated or supported, as it was in the Bush years, lots of school districts still teach it and haven't switched to a more comprehensive curriculum because they fear outcry and backlash from parents, communities, and religious groups. My own daughter brought home material from her class, talking about how porn causes sex crimes, and is the equivalent of heroin. Ultimately, they're making kids suffer, and feeding the fear of sex.

So, it's on you. Inoculate your son or daughter against the risks of porn. Vaccinate them, dammit. Not by showing them porn—though you could. Over the years, millions of dads and stepdads and uncles gave teenage boys porn magazines. And now, those boys are senators and presidents, priests and mechanics, husbands and father, criminals, saints, and prisoners, just like all the rest of us.

Educate your kids about risks, like the issue of child porn, and the risks of getting labelled a child pornographer if they distribute a naked pic of an under aged friend who sends it to them. But don't only talk about the negatives and risks. Acknowledge the positives in porn, that it can be sexy and fun. If you don't, you're just replicating the failure of the Just Say No drug campaigns.

Talk to them about real sex, about relationships, about respect, about communication and negotiation. Teach them how to be responsible adults, who understand, accept and own their sexuality and their choices. Start, and continue, a dialogue with your teens about sexual health, relationships, integrity, and respect. If you don't, you can't help prepare your child for the world around them, a world that involves porn.

Teenage Boys and Extreme Porn

Dan Savage once shared with me a letter he received from a concerned mom. She had found out that her son was watching really violent porn with gangbangs, BDSM, and extreme domination toward women. The mom was really bothered by this and got even more upset when she found out that her teenage boy had very negative, misogynistic attitudes about girls and how they should just "give up sex" to the guy.

This is a very good example of why porn, especially violent and BDSM porn, is made for adults and not for teens. This material is sophisticated and intense, and requires maturity to understand and incorporate it. While I am against censorship, I do think it is important to recognize that these portrayals can be confusing and even warping, when they are viewed by kids who haven't received effective, pragmatic, and real-world sex education. When we tell kids, "Just say no to sex," and don't talk to them about the weird, wild world of grown-up freaky sex that's out there, this is exactly the kind of confused kids we get.

I encourage parents to have dialogues with kids about what's out there, to discuss it in advance, so when the kids encounter it, they can talk to the parents about it, their feelings and values. It's critically important that the parents share their values and attitudes about sex, porn, and relationships with their kids.

When it comes to such porn—that is misogynistic or violent—it's a priority that the parents share how that kind of porn makes the mom feel as a woman. The father's encouragement and participation in this conversation is critical. Often the dad can sound like he's minimizing it, and the mom is catastrophizing it. Parents need to be on a shared page when they talk with their son. Not to shame or guilt trip the kid, but to help him understand the real people issues con-

nected to that material. It's important in these conversations to help teens understand the difference between fantasy and real life. It's probably fine to fantasize about this stuff, but enacting it in real life is more complicated and risky. Explain to him that acting these ways in real life is likely to hurt others, as well as yourself, and to even result in legal problems.

The popularity of *Fifty Shades of Grey* led to lots of women, including teen girls, wanting to try BDSM, bondage, and spanking. Unfortunately, it's also led to numerous situations where males and females got into complex areas of sex and consent that they weren't ready for. Dealing with these issues requires sophisticated boundaries, communication, and negotiation that adults struggle with. Teens are ill-prepared to manage these waters safely. I call this Varsity level sex and it takes maturity. And unfortunately, *Fifty Shades of Grey* doesn't depict a good model for how to practice this sex ethically or responsibly.

I've talked about these kinds of issues with both my son and daughter, and numerous patients, in different ways, appropriate to their ages and gender. It's scary stuff but the best approach is a balanced one. If you demonize porn, the kid will keep their use secret. If you don't acknowledge that some material is scary and confusing, the kid won't understand their feelings when they run into it.

I believe men have a responsibility to model respect, integrity, responsibility, and sexual self-acceptance for other males.

Unfortunately, many young men today have few good role models. If there's not a dad in the life of that teen boy, I encourage moms to try to find a surrogate male if the mom doesn't feel comfortable talking about these issues. Ask your male friends to talk to your son, man to man, about these issues and help that teen boy learn about themselves, about sexuality, and about relationships. It's important. If you ignore it, these things can get worse.

I've seen young men who struggle with tremendous shame and guilt over very normal levels of masturbation, porn use, or feelings of aggression, lust, and anger, when these young men were raised without that kind of adult male support and role modeling. It certainly doesn't happen all the time, but when young men are raised without healthy male role models, it's tough for those young men to learn to how to deal effectively with some of the darker sides of masculinity.

If we don't talk to teen males about what sex is in porn versus real life, then like all teen boys, they will think they know everything they need to know.

Opting In or Out: Preventing Children from Seeing Porn

One of the current debates about porn is whether to mandate processes that require either age verification or "opting-in" to view pornography. The large volume of pornography on the Internet can have a, if not clearly harmful, at least a confusing impact on teens who don't have the experience or knowledge to handle this information in a mature way. Like R-rated movies or weapons, Internet pornography should be limited by age, just as print or hard-copy porn is.

That all sounds good, and I agree. In theory. Unfortunately, in most places where this has been tried or proposed, it is usually done so in the model of "SAVE THE KIDS!" with a panicked presentation that says porn is destroying kids. Frankly, I think that's ridiculous and demeaning to teens. Lots of teens can handle this information more maturely than many religiously conservative adults. It's also an immensely bad idea. Telling a teen that something is taboo is a guarantee to draw their eye.

Whenever someone suggests these opt-in/age-verification strategies to me, I always quote Admiral Akbar: "IT'S A TRAP!" Let me ask you two simple questions:

1. What material, specifically, are you going to require age verification or opting in for? It's not so simple as to say, "Porn." Because there are no clear, reliable definitions of what porn, or obscenity, actually is. So, how is it decided, specifically, what material qualifies?

2. Who in the government, specifically, do you trust enough to decide what material you can see without age-verification, opting-in, or tracking? How do you know you can trust them to make that decision for you, for your kids? And how do you know you can keep trusting them? What measures would you need to put in place to ensure they don't become an arm of the government, censoring material for political reasons?

That's the deal. In the UK when they tried this, they just coincidentally ended up requiring "opt-in" on material that included sex education, mental health issues, and discussions of being gay or lesbian. When Google put an age restriction in place on a kids' search engine, it restricted access to information about issues related to sexual orientation and identity. Do you REALLY trust the government, or a large corporation, to decide what's good for you? Or, the moralistic busybodies who are campaigning for these restrictions? Because trust me, their definition of sexual health or obscenity is different than yours is. If you're really concerned about teens in your home seeing pornography, you can install filtering software yourself. But be prepared that it doesn't always work, and stuff slips through. Savvy teens can get by it, just the same way teens have gotten booze, guns, cigarettes, porn magazines, and all kinds of things they weren't supposed to get.

You CAN check the browser history on your kids' computers to see what they're looking at. Be prepared though. One friend checked her kid's computer and found websites for smoking fetish porn and cheerleader gangbang porn. Turned out, it wasn't her kid watching, but the kid's grandparents. The grandmother liked the smoking porn, and the granddad liked watching young cheerleaders get gangbanged. Neither one knew how to clear the browser. And each was watching the porn in secrecy while the other grandparent was at church with the kid. Too bad they didn't talk with each other about their interests. I'm sure they could find some smoking cheerleader gangbang porn out there. . . .

Reshaping
the Porn
Industry

So, if we follow Annie Sprinkle's advice, and tried to make "better" porn more accessible, to counteract the "bad" porn, how would we do that? One of the most important ways, is for us to start listening to people who make porn, who star in porn, and who actually research porn, as opposed to letting our dialogue be driven by those who hate and fear porn.

Porn Star Infatuation

Porn stars and adult performers have told me that one of the risks they face in life and career is that they might be stalked or raped by an obsessed fan. Many performers have experienced sad, scary interactions with people online, and in person, who either attack them for their sexual career or decide that their sexual career means they will have sex with anyone. During the trial of an MMA fighter charged with violently beating up his porn-star girlfriend, the defense argued that because the girlfriend was in porn, she really shouldn't have been bothered by the violence or aggression from her boyfriend.

As our society and media treats porn as though it is shameful, they are also treating porn performers as though they themselves are shameful. When we allow this, it diminishes porn performers and leaves us treating them as though they have fewer rights or protections compared to other people.

But beyond such scary, violent, and criminal interactions, porn performers also get nervous about the line where a loyal, dedicated fan crosses from being a fan to being a stalker. It's fine to get really hot and bothered over your favorite porn star.

Something about them just really pushes your buttons. But don't be a stalker, dude.

Porn performers today are more accessible to their fans than ever before. If you are infatuated with a certain performer, that's understandable. These are beautiful, sexy people, who share something incredibly intimate and allow you to witness it. You can follow your favorite performer on social media. Let them know how much you like the work they do. Performers of every type love to hear this kind of thing from their fans. It fans the flames of their careers and their confidence.

Pay to join their website, where you can see videos they're in and know that the money you pay to watch the video is going right into their sexy little pocket. Lots of performers maintain Amazon wish lists. You can buy them something they want. Often they will post a picture of them wearing the item you gifted as a way of saying thanks to you, specifically.

Many performers travel, dancing or speaking around the country. You can keep up with them that way and maybe even meet them in person. Some performers even work as escorts or are star guest performers at Nevada brothels. You might get luckier than you ever dreamed.

There's nothing wrong with your fantasies and dreams. People have fantasized about sexy stars since the days of silent films. **But remember these are daydreams.** These are fantasies you can indulge. But don't get confused about the ways these fantasies reflect your idea of reality or impact your conscious behavior.

Don't be a stalker. Don't go to performers' homes, send threatening messages, or invade people's privacy. People who do that go to jail. I shouldn't have to say that. But porn performers get stalked, threatened and even hurt by crazed fans. Don't be that guy.

Porn performers get harassed online and in person. Banks

sometimes refuse to take their money because of the ways they earned it. A few years ago, someone hacked a medical clinic that provided STI testing to porn performers and released their real names online, along with their addresses and names of their family members. These are hateful acts that suggest porn performers don't deserve the privacy or rights that anyone else would have. That's disgusting.

Porn performers are playing a role. It's a role that you find appealing and that means something. What is it in their role that touches you? Is it their confident sexuality? Their obvious enjoyment and fun during sex? Their assertiveness or their submissiveness? Whatever it is, these are clues to you of things that you want in your life, in your bed and relationship. Use this to understand yourself and your needs, and learn how to seek those qualities out in people in your life. Communicate these needs to your partners, your wife, girlfriend, or husband.

When you find someone like this in your life, send a thank you to that performer who inspired you. They love that. And they deserve those thank yous.

Amateur Porn: A Healthier "Free-Range" Alternative?

A part of the ethical porn movement includes an elevation and celebration of amateur porn. There's an idea that amateur porn is inherently consensual and better demonstrates real-world sex. I like amateur porn myself, don't get me wrong. Amateur porn is one of the things I like to watch on tube sites, because it's easy for people to upload their own self-made videos, and let others enjoy them. But I think there are some people who are fooling themselves over what amateur porn is and isn't.

If you regularly take herbal supplements, eat organic foods, and avoid GMOs, then yes, I can assure you that amateur, indie, and ethical porn is definitely better for you. It injects fewer toxins into your sexuality and leaves your skin feeling nice and fresh. You should definitely be shopping for organic porn.

For the rest of us—amateur porn is a tradeoff. There's somewhat more chance that what you are seeing is "real," in that it is relatively unscripted and closer to reality, reflecting the type of sex that the actors might have on a regular basis, whether the camera is there or not. But, remember that porn is a fantasy, which, by definition, involves an escape from reality. Also remember that sometimes "real" sex involves people faking orgasms.

Professional porn works to give you better lighting, better camera work, and production value. The performers are screened and made up so that you might see fewer zits and ingrown hairs. They are actors, they have to be to maintain enthusiasm, passion and erections while the directors are doing retakes, still shots, and telling them to move in awkward positions so the camera gets a better view.

But most porn performers are in porn because they like sex, especially adventurous sex. Sure, they need the money. It's a job. But like the luckiest of us, many of them are in the job because they enjoy what they do. There's a good chance that they're enjoying what they're doing as they are filmed.

There's lots of semi-pro "amateur" camgirls and camguys, who enjoy getting on camera and being sexy. Most of them are independent, and such venues offer them more freedom, control, and often a better portion of profits. But, you can't make assumptions about amateur camgirls/camguys any more than you can make such assumptions about any other kind of amateur porn.

Amateur porn MIGHT offer you greater chances of seeing sex by people who are really into it and doing it for fun, rather than just money. But the porn industry has caught onto the success of "people next door porn," and lots of the amateur porn you see out there, is in fact "semi-pro." These are people who don't do porn as their main job, but they're not exactly doing it for free either. So, if you believe reality television is real, then you go right ahead and enjoy the hell out of your reality amateur porn.

A danger with amateur porn is that you can't easily verify and ensure that the actors are participating consensually and of legal age. It could easily be something like revenge porn. Any of that could be a problem, both ethically and legally. Some of the user-upload sites now have numbers of "confirmed/verified" amateur performers, to overcome this issue.

Folks like Cindy Gallop argue that we need more porn that is less fantasy-based and more reflective of sexual realities, in order to help people (especially young people and young men) have a better idea what real sex versus porn sex looks like. I agree a lot with this idea, though I think we also need to value and accept the fantasy in porn, the same way we accept fantasy elsewhere. In real life, orgasms take work, negotiation and communication. If that is sexy for you, amateur porn is where you are more likely to find it. But you might have to wade through an awful lot of bad, unwatchable, unattractive, and unsexy material to find what you are looking for.

Gay Male Ethical Porn

The debate over ethical porn is largely housed in porn production that involves female performers. There's very little dialogue about ethics in porn involving gay men. Why is that?

First, men, including gay men, are seen as needing to "suck it up" (sorry, couldn't resist) when it comes to ethics and consent. There's the myth that men can't really be raped—a dangerous, discounting myth that pervades debates about rape and consent.

There's also the simple fact that people who are not gay men often try to avoid thinking about, or even acknowledging, that gay male porn exists. Gay male porn has always posed a challenge to many of the anti-porn arguments, particularly when they come from feminist perspectives, arguing that porn is degrading toward women. The fact that men are "degraded" in gay male porn is ignored as irrelevant.

Some of this comes down to the gendered nature of the debates over sex and consent and rape. There's a long, long history of men raping and sexually abusing women. Ethical porn producers want to protect women's rights and worry that without such protections, women in porn will be treated poorly. Men, and male sexuality, is seen as less in need of protection. Female sexuality, even when it is aggressive, is perceived as less threatening.

One female porn performer and producer told me that prior to our conversation about this, she'd never thought of these issues before, or about the ways gender, consent, and ethics were intertwined in porn. She recounted tales of having consent and physical boundaries violated by other women in porn, and at porn conventions, but that such issues were really of little concern and didn't "seem" like actual violations. Women commonly grab each other's breasts or butts at such events without asking for the consent they would demand from men doing so. On-set, she said male performers often get little attention, in terms of their needs, their interests, or perhaps, even their consent. "There are many male performers or wannabes out there," she said. "We don't have to really protect them as a commodity as much as we do female performers." In porn, as well as in real life, men are seen as disposable. Even in BDSM scenes, where she is filming female dominant, male submissive scenes, she acknowledged that she worries more about the needs, feelings, and consent of the female dominant versus the male submissive performer.

Gay, lesbian, and queer porn is often a first step toward people experiencing and acknowledging their own sexuality. In that, such porn should be the material we protect most strongly, as it starts the work of heal-ing the wounds of stigma, shame, and discrimination.

Gay male and trans performers and porn producers ARE concerned about the issues of STI testing, privacy, and piracy. But these performers are often so socially stigmatized for their sexuality and orientation that the porn environment may feel very affirmative and accepting— even when there are cases and examples where such

performers are not treated ethically, or where isolation, depression and drug use associated with their porn performances negatively affect their mental health. It's my hope that as the ethical porn dialogue and movement progresses, gay male and trans performers will be included. They deserve to have their voices heard and to have their needs and rights considered in these debates.

Porn Can Be Feminist and Support Female Empowerment

Some people, both men and women, are feminists who feel guilty watching porn because they worry about the "girls" in the porn. They get upset when guys do things in the porn like hit the performers with their dicks. They feel like that kind of porn is inherently misogynistic. Certainly, many of the anti-porn activists like Gail Dines have shouted that acts such as gagging, moneyshots, and spanking in porn are violent evidence of hatred of women. These images aren't new to modern porn, but exist in the historical record, in vintage porn and petroglyphs.

Responsible men and women should support equality for women and support women to be treated well and fairly. But, we have to watch out for our assumptions. It's sweet when men want to protect and treasure women. I often do too. It's gentlemanly. But some women want men to slap their face with their dicks, and want to be tied up and taken. They might want to pretend to be raped. They might love being looked at in a lustful manner.

And they don't need or want your well-intended protectiveness. They're big girls. They can tell you if they want you to watch their backs.

Modern feminism is in a positive place, moving society forward toward a point where many women now have the freedom to choose how they want to be, and how they want to explore their sexuality. They might want to be an empowered dominant, they may choose an egalitarian relationship of equality, and they might desire to be empowered in their sexuality by fulfilling their fantasies of being treated like a serving girl wench of the Middle Ages. I think that's all pretty damn amazing. And sexy.

The question is, can you watch that performer get slapped or choked on a guy's dick, masturbate to it, enjoy it, but do so in a respectful, ethical manner? Maybe. If we have some reasonable belief that she's there doing it by her own choice. If we support as men, and as a society, her right to choose what she wants in that situation.

Now, an even better question is whether you can do this in real life? Can an ethical, responsible guy, a gentleman, slap a lover with his penis? That's a fun question to think about. I don't know what the answer is because it depends on how that man views sex, his penis, his partner, how he does this, and what he does before and after. How do you answer this? What would make the answer yes or no?

For me, I think a lot of it depends on whether you've asked that woman whether she likes that kind of thing. If you've never asked her about it, and you slap her in the face with your dick, then you're behaving like a jackass. If you've talked with her about it, and she says, "Yeah, that's kind of hot and dirty and makes me tingle," then you're being a loving, responsible, and Good, Giving and Game partner.

How to Know Ethical Porn When You See It

When I go to the grocery store, I can't tell the difference between "fair trade" coffee and coffee that came from a company that treats its farmers poorly. I have to trust the labelling and trust that people are working to make sure those labels don't lie. Right now, there's no easy way to tell when porn is made ethically. There's no "This Porn Was Made Ethically!" stickers. Maybe there should be. But until that happens, it's difficult for the average consumer of porn to be able to tell if porn is made responsibly or ethically.

But just because it's difficult to tell doesn't mean you're off the hook for responsibility. You can still enjoy porn and work to try to find material that was made in a way that supports ethical practices, responsible sex, and doesn't make you feel guilty. It takes a bit of work and effort, and it might cost a monthly fee, versus getting free porn. But, it's important work to do, and it's worth the effort. It matters.

If you paid for the porn, then chances are better (not guaranteed) that it's more likely to be porn you can trust, in terms of legality. But, usually, you need to be paying the producer or the performer themselves. Some of the tube/aggregator sites charge for VIP membership, but they may still show you porn that is pirated from porn producers.

Aggregators like tube sites don't currently have to maintain records of ages or consent. So watching porn on such sites makes it so that you're uncertain if those performers consented and were treated fairly. Sites like Vivid, Pink Visual, and Kink.Com are a few that produce high-quality material and work hard to ensure that they are legally and ethically compliant. Often, these companies do something clever and have interviews with the porn performers after the video, where they talk about consent as well as what the performers got out of the experience. Those clips will go a long way toward relieving your guilt.

Is it porn that lets the performer have a voice? Are there interviews or comments from the performer that give you an idea of what they want or what they're getting?

All ethical porn doesn't necessarily involve nice sex. Some ethical porn can involve rough sex and be just as kinky or aggressive as other forms of porn. But, only if that's what the performer consented to and agrees to. So, are there any cues in the video, or the site, that they make sure they get consent, willingness, and agreement from the performers?

Similarly, ethical porn doesn't have to have condoms. Condoms are a big debate in porn these days, and some ethical porn producers require them. A growing number of porn groups use a "double-blind" strategy in their scenes. In this process, performers are asked anonymously before the scene if they want condoms used. If anyone says yes, the scene is shot as a condom scene, no questions asked. This can be tough for the viewer/consumer to identify. It's one reason again, why you need to find people you trust, who know the "ins-and-outs" of the porn industry and can tell you who out there is being ethical around safe sex. Some of these folks are listed in the resources section at the end of this book.

Porn made commercially in the United States, Canada, Scandinavia, Europe, or the UK is more likely to be legally safer, though it depends on the company as to how they treat their performers. If it is made in these areas, it's likely made under pretty stringent and enforced laws ensuring consent, documentation of age, etc. If it's not, you might not know what you are getting, or what the performers experienced as it was made. That's not to say that only porn made in the First World is ethical, but it stands a better chance of passing the litmus test.

Amateur porn is a tough one. But with real amateur porn, you may not know whether it's ethical or not. Amateur porn is often on aggregator sites, uploaded by users. There's little to no information about ages, consent, or anything else. So, we are left to rely on our assessment of the performers. Do they appear into it? Are there verbal signs of consent? In the video, who appears to hold the power? Any signs of force, abuse, or impairment that might take away consent? Do the people in the video appear adult? I tell people they should avoid any "teen amateur" porn like the plague. If there's any chance the performers are actually under age, you might as well be pouring gasoline on your dick and masturbating using that as lube. You are literally playing with fire and supporting the chances that underage people are being taken advantage of.

Webcamming is one type of porn that is somewhat more likely to be "more" ethical. In this, you are interacting with a performer online as they chat and do a show. Depending on the website used, 50 percent or more of the money you pay for the show goes straight to the performer. Performers are usually independent, and semi-pro. Performers are usually in charge of their own performance, deciding how and where their limits are. But some audience members can be bullying and inappropriate toward the performer. Often, other audience members like yourself take the steps to enforce politeness and respect of the performer.

You're more likely to find ethical porn when it is made by people who embrace the labels of feminist porn, indie porn, and queer porn. Female and LGBT porn producers, as well as those not associated with mainstream porn industry, are more likely to make porn in a way that respects the rights of the performers in a legally and in a non-exploitative manner.

Nate Glass runs the organization called Takedown Piracy, which works under contract to porn stars and content producers, to prevent unauthorized piracy of porn videos as well as video games. When his firm identifies ongoing piracy, they take action to address it and ensure the website takes down the pirated material. Nate tells me that:

It's hard for the average consumer to tell the difference

between pirated and legal authorized content. This is done purposely by pirates because they know saying "this is pirated material" will turn off some potential viewers. My advice is that if you aren't pulling out your credit card and paying for the content, there's a good chance you might be watching pirated content.

Takedown Piracy has a list of piracy free sites you can visit, where they have safe, legal content. You can also report pirated materials to Takedown Piracy at http://takedownpiracy.com/tips. You can also report these videos or images to the porn star. They truly appreciate you looking out for them and protecting their image and business.

In the videos you watch, or the camming you view/interact with, were the performers paid, and paid well, for the hard work they do? This is tough to tell as a viewer. So, the best way to support this is to advocate that all porn performers should be well-paid for their work. If the whole industry were forced to treat people well and pay for their labor appropriately, we'd have a lot fewer issues. Until then, at the end of this book are some groups who are known currently to make ethical porn where performers are treated well, have consented, and have the right to stand up for their needs and wishes. You can look at these groups, and you can look for recommendations by these folks to find porn you can trust.

Ethical Porn and Sexual Health

Are porn producers ethically responsible to contribute to better sexual health in the world? That's a big, loaded question, and a challenging controversy. This is the question that people are asking, and answering for themselves, when they challenge modern porn for having violence, spanking, extreme BDSM, simulated rape, and other aspects of the dark side of sex and humanity. The United Kingdom is wrestling with this issue right now, even expressing concern that the popularity of porn is increasing rates of anal sex in teens. They are probably right. Porn HAS increased the commonness of anal sex, pubic shaving, and male on female oral sex. Would the world, and sex, be better if porn didn't include those elements? Would our world be healthier and our sexuality be "nicer" if porn didn't present those elements?

I think not. I think history is clear that these elements, even the darker ones, are part of our sexuality, part of humanity. Wishing them away doesn't work and neither does pretending they don't exist. Even if commercial porn didn't include that material and those scenes, people would still want them and seek them out—and thus, an underground, illegal world of porn would grow up in response. And we are all very clear that an underground, illegal, unmonitored porn industry is far more dangerous, and far less ethical, than one where transparency exists.

We should hold porn producers, where we can identify them, responsible to be ethical in promoting sexual health. But, I'm pretty sure that my definitions of sexual health are different than that of most of the opponents of pornography. Because I truly believe that even some of these most intense, extreme, challenging aspects of sexuality CAN be healthy. Sexual health includes pleasure, self-determination, self-acceptance, authenticity, honesty, and most of all, freedom. I don't believe that sexual health is possible in a culture that does not protect sexual freedom.

The World Health Organization declares that sexual health is:

> The state of physical, emotional, mental and social well-being related to sexuality; it is not merely the absence of disease, dysfunction and infirmity. Sexual health requires a positive, respectful approach to sexuality and sexual relationships, as well as the possibility of having pleasurable and safe sexual experiences, free of coercion, discrimination and violence. For sexual health to be attained and maintained, the sexual rights of all persons must be respected, protected and fulfilled.

Pornography can and should do a much better job of highlighting consent and lack of coercion, even in that material which is fantasy. But what pornography already does very well is respect the sexual right of self-determination. Pornography, by its very nature, respects an individual's right to be turned on by the fantasy portrayed in that material. By producing that material, pornographers are saying to their audience, "*You are allowed, encouraged, to be turned on by this.*"

Like it or not, the porn industry has been a champion of sexual freedom. From Larry Flynt's famous trials to the role that gay porn has played in the lives of LGBT living in secrecy and shame, porn has been at the frontlines of our fight to ensure sexual freedom and self-determination. Illegal, hidden, secret, and morally challenging porn has been an avenue for people who seek sexual freedom in a society that does not agree that they deserve it. For many, porn is their first exposure to the idea, the possibility, that their secret sexual desires don't have to be secret, and that they are not alone in holding them. These are the first, most powerful steps toward freedom—coming out of the shadows and joining forces.

It's why I think our job, as porn consumers, is to stand up and acknowledge sexual diversity and tell people to keep their moral judgments out of our private, consensual sexual decisions.

Growing an Ethical Porn Industry

This book is mostly about how we, as men, can use porn ethically and responsibly. But we also have an obligation to advocate that the porn industry make itself better. Financially, the more we support and encourage ethical porn, the more it will be available.

We can also tell the porn industry that we want more options for ethical porn. Look at the way the agriculture and food production industry is responding to people's desire for "organic" food, or for non-GMO food. Because the public is expressing lots of vocal concerns, and expressing those concerns with their wallets and credit cards, the industry has responded. The more we assert these demands as consumers—to the porn industry, and in opposition to unethical, illegal, or pirated materials—the more chance we have to force the many aspects of the porn industry to shift.

The porn industry is not a "monolithic" beast, run by organized crime, where we need to convince just a few people. The porn industry is more like the Hydra, with many heads. That's not to say the porn industry is a monster. I truly think it's not. Most of these people are business people like the rest of us, trying to turn a profit in a cold, unforgiving and deeply unsympathetic world. The way you change business practices is by affecting the revenue spreadsheets. When porn companies and websites see ethical porn producers and practices generating money and revenues, they will shift in that direction. Cindy Gallop calls this "competitive collaboration," calling for people in the porn industry to come together and collaborate to make things better for everyone.

When they do, in order for us to support them, it's important for the producers of porn to convey their ethical stance and practices to us as consumers. This way, we know what we are getting and can relax into our sexual pleasure, content that the performers we are watching were treated fairly and ethically.

Write the porn companies who make the porn you watch and ask them whether they are an ethical business, treating their performers well. The more questions they get, asking how they treat their performers and if they are ethical as they make porn, the more they see that consumers of porn care about these issues. This will lead to more pressure for porn companies to publicly adopt ethical practices.

Just recently, some of the online tube site/porn aggregators have begun to change some of their practices, taking these issues into consideration. Some of them are now:

- Conducting age/identity verifications with amateur submissions, offering greater safety and legal protections for viewers and makers alike;
- Partnering with porn producers, and using legal teaser material, with links back to the producer's website;
- Creating sexual wellness and education categories on their sites, and acknowledging their role as an introduction to sexuality for many viewers.

Porn isn't going to go away. It's a part of human sexuality and has been for as long as we've had genitalia and something to draw with. Fear of pornography is the key obstacle here, as shame, blame, and fear keep us from addressing the real issues in pornography use. It's simply too easy to ignore the person and focus on the porn.

It's far easier for politicians and moral groups to attack and demonize porn, rather than addressing the complicated issues involved in:

- Modern, real-world sex education for teens that prepares them not just for sex, but for sex and life in a world our grandparents never imagined
- Gender differences about sex
- What gender and sexual orientation means, in the modern world
- How to adapt laws and society to accommodate these changing attitudes towards sex, and growing acceptance of sexual diversity
- Male difficulties in seeking help coping with emotions and loss
- Stigma toward sex and sex work
- Shaming and stigmatizing of rape victims
- Acknowledging the wide world of sexual diversity

- Whether people's sexual predilections truly mean anything about who they are as a person
- Moral opposition to non-heteronormative sexuality and relationships
- The people who are living in pain, or lost to suicide, because they cannot reconcile their sexual desires with the moral values of the culture they were raised in

All of these issues are critical for our society to continue to address, but porn is merely a scapegoat, and worse, a distraction.

The more we work together to make porn better, more ethical, and more responsible, the more we can personally be ethical and responsible in our own use of porn. In this way, we can help our society to have real, effective conversations about sex and gender. We can force real conversations about what porn is and isn't. We need to move beyond the blaming and shaming of porn and start talking about our need for real sex education, about the needs men have to enjoy sexuality on their terms, and about why men have so much difficulty coping with negative emotions. We need to enjoin conversations about the conflicts between our increasing social acceptance of sexual diversity, versus moral and religious opposition to sexual freedoms. We need to have discussions and definitions of sexual health that include people's use of porn to explore their own sexuality and to learn what they like and what their libidos respond to. As long as we are focused on porn, we're missing the target. The point of this book is to refocus our attention away from the fear games and toward the things we really need to talk about. This is the only way we can help the people truly suffering, whether porn is involved or not.

Afterword

Notes from an Ethical Porn Performer

Chanel Preston

"Are you addicted to sex?"

Feeling deflated, I looked at the young college student who asked me this question, and I simply replied, "No."

I had spent ninety minutes discussing the stigma and discrimination porn performers regularly face. I talked about my background growing up in Alaska, and how close I remain with my family despite my chosen career path. I mentioned being a founder and the president of a nonprofit organization that aims to help protect the rights and safety of performers. We discussed the legislative work that organization does, how it focuses on educating performers in their rights and skills. Not least, I explained why I chose to be recorded in sexually explicit performances: I told the students how my career in porn has allowed me to explore myself sexually in ethical and healthy ways. Since I relish every chance to talk about sexual freedom and the problems facing sexually explicit performers, it was no surprise that when the student asked if I was addicted to sex, a dispirited "no" was all I could muster. Even after all I had addressed, the stigma surrounding those of us who choose a career in pornography remained undeterred.

I am often asked to speak at universities and colleges.

Talking about porn and sexuality is one of the things I enjoy most about being a porn star. I look forward to debunking myths, challenging stereotypes, and demystifying the world of sex. Sadly, I am regularly disappointed in how little the students know about their sexuality, and it concerns me that education about sex is being withheld. An education would give students the tools they need to protect their personal safety, flourish interpersonally, and see through inaccuracies the media (even porn) perpetuates. College students are adults who are out on their own and making choices for themselves; as sexual beings, they deserve better.

When it comes to sex, unfortunately, people are prone to make inaccurate assumptions not only about others but, even more, about themselves. People of all genders ask me what it means for them to enjoy porn or like a certain type of sex. Are they addicts? Fetishists? As they prepare for a porn star fantasy analysis, I usually say, "Nothing. Your fantasies probably mean nothing." They look back at me, and I think I can read their minds. "How could this be? Fantasies invoke such strong feelings in me! These are acts I would NEVER perform in real life—and I can barely even mention them in public! They must mean something." My retort is direct: "People think about things they would never do in real life ALL the time, and they don't believe they mean anything significant. Why would sexual fantasies be any different?" Think of the times you have experienced strong emotions—anger, fear, or sadness—and a thought crossed your mind that you could never admit. Maybe someone made you angry, and you felt an urge to punch the person in the face; maybe you imagined driving someone off the road because they cut you off. We deem such thoughts normal because we know that, in real life, we will not conduct ourselves in this way. In the safe container of our own minds, it is less satisfying to consider the reality than it is to enjoy the fantasy. Since we separate reality and fantasy in other areas of life, why can't we in our sexual lives?

Our sexual fantasies do not recognize the boundaries that we normally function within every day, so it is no surprise that we may find ourselves fantasizing about something that seems out of character, weird, or even illegal. If fantasies followed the same rules we follow in our everyday life, they would not be fantasies. If you find yourself thinking about things that you would not do in real life, feel comfortable knowing that the safest place to explore these fantasies is in your head. And if you do find that you want to explore outside of your head, then there are plenty of safe ways to go about it. One of these ways to watch, literally, a fantasy play out in reality is in pornography. It is my job as a performer to re-create what I can imagine you wanting to see in your head. Even if it's morbid, strange, scary, or boring, I re-create these fantasies because I know they exist; and by watching porn, people can *safely* explore their desires. So, instead of asking yourself what your desires mean, simply ask yourself what your desires are, and then explore them. As a porn star, I love what I do most when it makes people feel good, not guilty.

Now, I am not a psychologist, and I did not utilize scientific method to reach conclusions that fantasies mean nothing—indeed, for a number of people, they might. But just as you wouldn't assume you were going to become a sociopath because you fantasized about throwing your neighbor down the stairs for playing loud music at three in the morning, you shouldn't assume your sexual fantasies are a sign that you are a horrible and doomed person. Our minds, as well as our sexuality, are fascinating, and sometimes confusing, systems to navigate—and sadly, most of us have not been given tools to do so safely and optimally. Without the tools to navigate sexuality, it is easy to make up stories about what our desires or sources of pleasure mean.

Ethical Porn for Dicks supplies essential tools for you to see your sexuality in another way. It replaces fear and shame with acceptance and discovery. It may be hard for many of us to embrace sexuality more positively because most of us have been told about all the risks and dangers that sex involves. But whatever those are, sex remains a natural part of life, and forcefully restricting our sexual feelings only damages our health. *Ethical Porn for Dicks* provides us with an understanding of sexual health that includes pornography.

Although it may seem like I am advocating for the use of porn, I am not. I am aware that porn is *not* as enjoyable to some as it is to others. I understand and respect that feeling, too. What I *am* advocating for is the exploration of our sexual desires.

After speaking to a class of students, I often find them relieved to notice they can change their views on sex and pornography, and still feel normal. Many of them walk out the door questioning all they thought they knew about sex, but not all of them; some students continue to see their sexuality as something that needs to be restricted. When the college student asked if I was addicted to sex, I doubt he knew the question revealed much about his own fears and anxieties. Although the student meant no harm, I knew that if he could entertain such an assumption about me, then he probably made a similar assumption about himself. I knew that, as a young man who undoubtedly has fantasies and has likely seen porn, he would never feel entirely comfortable with sex until he can expand his own self-imposed limitations.

If you believe people appear in porn because of an addiction to sex or the like, you will never respect our choice to perform; and if you don't respect our choice to perform, you will never respect yourself as a consumer of porn. Not respecting the use of pornography as sexual entertainment reflects a widespread misunderstanding that porn comes from a place without dignity or agency, and that porn use is seen as a shameful indulgence. That is simply not true. I am convinced it is possible to make and watch porn while remaining—perhaps becoming even more— perfectly safe and sane. The sooner we recognize that many beliefs about sex are products of fear and confusion, the sooner we can use fantasies and porn as ethical and healthy ways to explore our sexual lives more fully.

Research

References

These are the books and research articles I specifically cite in this book. See the next section for the researchers and writers who've influenced my thinking and understanding.

Baumeister, R.F., and J.M. Twenge, 2002. "The cultural suppression of female sexuality," *Review of General Psychology* 6(2), 166-203.

Danoff, Dudley. 2011. *Penis Power: The Ultimate Guide to Male Sexual Health*. Del Monaco Press, Beverly Hills, CA.

Flynt, Larry. 2004. *Sex, Lies and Politics: The Naked Truth*. Kensington Press. New York, NY.

Friday, Nancy. 1981. *Men in Love: Men's Sexual Fantasies: The Triumph of Love over Rage*. Dell Publishing, New York, NY.

Grubbs, J.B., J.J. Exline, K.I. Pargament, J.N. Hook, and R.D. Carlisle. 2015. "Transgression as addiction: religiosity and moral disapproval as predictors of perceived addiction to pornography," *Archives of Sexual Behavior* 44(1), 125-36.

Grubbs, J.B., N. Stauner, J.J. Exline, K.I. Pargament, and M. Lindberg. 2015. "Perceived addiction to internet pornography and psychological distress: examining relationships concurrently and over time," *Psychology of Addictive Behaviors* 29(4):1056-67.

James, E.L. 2012. *Fifty Shades of Grey*. Vintage Books, New York, NY.

Kahr, Brett. 2009. *Who's Been Sleeping in Your Head: The Secret World of Sexual Fantasies*. Basic Books. New York, NY.

Klein, Marty. 2012. *America's War on Sex: The Continuing Attack on Law, Lust, and Liberty*. Praeger. Westport, CT.

Lee, Jiz (ed). 2015. *Coming Out Like a Porn Star*. ThreeL Media. Berkeley, CA.

Ley, D. 2012. *The Myth of Sex Addiction*. Rowman and Littlefield. Lanham, MD.

Ley, D., J.M. Brovko, and R.C. Reid. 2015. "Forensic applications of 'sex addiction' in US legal proceedings," *Current Sexual Health Reports* 7(2), 108-16.

Ley, David. 2009. *Insatiable Wives: Women Who Stray and the Men Who Love Them*. Rowman and Littlefield. Lanham, MD.

Malan, Paul. 2015. "The Naked People in Your iPod." Available online at: https://medium.com/life-tips/the-naked-people-in-your-ipod-f770a27fdb59#.okb8cmcm4. Accessed February 16, 2016.

National Center for Missing and Exploited Children. http://www.cybertipline.com.

Offutt, Chris. 2016. *My Father, the Pornographer: A Memoir.* Atria Books. New York, NY.

Ogas, Ogi and Sai Gaddam. 2012. *A Billion Wicked Thoughts: What the Internet Tells Us about Sexual Relationships.* Plume. New York, NY.

Slifer, Dennis. 2000. *Serpent and the Sacred Fire: Fertility Images in Southwestern Rock Art.* University of New Mexico Press. Albuquerque, NM.

Stopes, Marie. 1918. *Married Love.* Available online at: http://digital.library.upenn.edu/women/stopes/married/1918.html. Accessed February 16, 2016.

Stulhofer, A., T. Jurin, and P. Briken. 2015. "Is high sexual desire a facet of male hypersexuality?" Results from an online study. *Journal of Sex and Marital Therapy.* November 16. Epub ahead of print.

Sullivan, Rebecca, and Alan McKee. 2015. *Pornography: Structures, Agency and Performance.* Polity Press. Cambridge, UK.

Vivas, Alison. 2013. *Making Peace with Porn: Adult Entertainment and Your Guy.* Hunter House. Alameda, CA.

Non-Porn Panic Researchers and Research-Driven Works on Porn

If you are looking for a therapist in your area who might not react negatively and with panic to your porn use or a therapist to help you and your wife resolve conflicts over porn, start by going to the website for the American Association of Sexuality Educators

Counselors and Therapists (AASECT). AASECT-certified counselors are far less likely to be ill-informed about porn or to react based on porn panic. Alternatively, if there's no one available in your area, look for therapists who work with LGBT issues. LGBT-informed therapists tend to be more accepting of sexual diversity and less prone to shame sexual expression. Finally, the National Coalition for Sexual Freedom is a nonprofit advocacy group that argues for the rights and needs of sexual diversity and sexual expression. They have a website where they list Kink Aware Professionals, including therapists who are supportive of sexual freedom.

If you want to understand where and how I support the things I talk about in this book—porn, its effects and impacts—start here. These researchers and writers are the sources I rely on to present the most honest guide to ethical porn that I can. I went to their writings, research and personal support, to try and understand how best to explain the current understanding of pornography and sexuality. There are many more than I can list. Research on sexuality, pornography, orientation and gender is a burgeoning field, with new research every day that is challenging assumptions.

Michael Aaron, Ph.D.—Michael is a New York therapist and sexologist with a background researching the links between childhood trauma and adult sexual difficulties. His book *Through the Keyhole: Debunking Our Biggest Sexual Myths and What It Means for Modern Relationships* is in the vein of much of my own writing career, challenging common moralistic and stigmatizing myths that affect shame and sexual insecurities.

Eric Anderson, Ph.D.—Eric is a sociologist, currently a professor in the UK at the University of Winchester. Eric started a career as the first openly gay high school track coach in the United States. He went on to publish about gay male professional athletes, nonmonogamy and male sexual fluidity. He argues strongly for attention to masculine sexuality.

Feona Attwood, Ph.D.—Feona is a media professor at Middlesex University (a joke that never gets old) in the UK. She is co-editor of *Porn Studies,* an academic journal examining pornography. She has published on the ways in which pornography and technology intersect.

Michael Bailey, Ph.D.—Northwestern University professor Mike Bailey has trained any number of influential current sexual researchers. Bailey instigated much of the modern research investigating sexual arousal in response to pornography, connected to sexual orientation. For many years, Bailey has moderated on online discussion group of the leading sexuality researchers and clinicians around the world. Participating in that discussion group is one of the most educational experiences I've ever had. Bailey is a controversial figure, with a standing conflict with parts of the trans community over his research and writing. But his research on arousal and identity contributes substantially to understanding of porn and its effects.

Sandra Byers, Ph.D.—Sandra is an Australian researcher and professor, doing excellent work studying technology, sexuality, cybersex and online sexual activities, in women and minorities.

James Cantor, Ph.D.—Canadian psychologist James Cantor is an excellent scientist whose work on pedophilia is provocative and forward thinking. Cantor and researchers under him have published excellent work on the typologies of people who present with porn or sex addiction claims. Cantor's work is consistently based upon the data and what these data actually show, versus what clinicians or theories predict.

Meredith Chivers, Ph.D.—Meredith is a researcher at Queens University in Canada and has conducted some remarkable research on female sexuality and female sexual arousal responses. Her research is most often misquoted and misunderstood to suggest that "all women are bisexual." Her research has furthered the understanding of female response to pornography more than almost anyone.

Cyndi Darnell, Ph.D.—Cyndi is an Australian therapist and sex educator. She has published work regarding ways to use pornography in a therapeutic manner within sexual therapy.

Lisa Diamond, Ph.D.—Lisa is a developmental psychologist at the University of Utah. Her work in sexual fluidity is stellar, leading to radical new understanding of the ways sexuality changes and morphs. Lisa once gave a presentation on male sexual fluidity, entitled "I Was Wrong," refuting her own past beliefs about the nonexistence of male sexual fluidity. That kind of scientific integrity is critical to move our understanding forward.

Milton Diamond, Ph.D.—Mickey Diamond is based in Hawaii and has an extensive career researching sexuality-related issues. His research showing the correlation between increased access to porn and decreased sexual violence should be critical and essential reading for anyone interested in social policy regarding these issues.

Chris Donaghue, Ph.D..—Chris is a writer, therapist and television personality who was originally trained in the sex addiction field. He broke away from it, and now argues that it is a shaming, unhealthy and antiquated model. His book *Sex Outside the Lines* is a marvelous book that challenges assumptions and biases about sex, gender, and relationships.

Katherine Frank, Ph.D.—Kate is an anthropologist whose dissertation involved a study of how men actually behave in strip clubs and the motivations and masculinity involved in their behaviors. She has also published on group sex and a host of other sexuality-related issues. I've described her book on group sex *Plays Well in Groups* as "the book I would have written if I got invited to orgies as much as Kate does."

Josh Grubb—Josh is a researcher at Case Western University currently. He has published ground-breaking work on the role of religious beliefs in porn addiction, the state of treatment of porn addiction, and the long-term effects of identifying as a porn addict. His work, more than anyone's, examines causality in this area and the connections between our internal experiences and the use of porn. Josh has forthcoming research in this area.

Amy Hasinoff, Ph.D.—Amy is a college professor in communications in Denver. Her book *Sexting Panic* explores the ways in which society's strong, frightened response to teen sexting has led to reactions that have penalized and criminalized girls.

Debby Herbenick, Ph.D.—Debby is a researcher, writer, lecturer, and media expert on sexuality. She has published countless works on sexuality, in both the academic and lay press, and is one of the best people out there in explaining complex, challenging issues around sexuality in an engaging, nonthreatening way.

Helen Hester, Ph.D.—at Middlesex University (nope, still not getting old) Helen is a young researcher exploring pornography use and the meaning of pornography. Her recent publication on female use of pornographic GIFs is brilliant.

Myles Jackman—Myles is a UK attorney who has been involved in the legal battles over access to porn in the United Kingdom. He's a brilliant, impassioned man dedicated to supporting sexual freedom and diversity, for both the makers and the viewers of porn.

Paul Joannides, Ph.D.—Paul is a dear friend and psychologist, whose graphically illustrated sexual manual *The Guide to Getting It On* is now in its eleventh edition, as he is constantly updating it with the most recent science and research. His YouTube videos are scientifically based, pragmatic advice, and intended to reduce fear and shame.

Robert King, Ph.D.—Robert is a psychologist and researcher in Ireland, who studies issues related to sexuality, pornography, and evolutionary psychology.

Marty Klein, Ph.D.—Dr. Marty Klein has been leading the fight against sexual shaming and arguing for good sexological science and policy for many years. He's written numerous books, with an upcoming one on porn. *America's War on Sex* is the simply the best exploration of our country's conflicted relationship with sexuality. His newsletter "Sexual Intelligence" is a fabulous way to stay on top of the current social debates about sex and the real science that should be informing them.

Joe Kort, Ph.D.—Joe is a Michigan therapist and writer who spent years working within the sex addiction model. He's now rejected it as a shaming paradigm that ignores many realities of human sexuality, and sexual diversity. His book *Is My Husband Gay, Straight, or Bi?*

explores the roles of male sexual fluidity and how pornography can play a part in these dynamics.

Justin Lehmiller, Ph.D.—Justin is a psychologist and Director of Social Psychology Graduate Program at Ball State (that joke never gets old either). Justin writes for *Playboy* and published a textbook *The Psychology of Human Sexuality*.

Brian McNair—Australian researcher and media commentator, Brian McNair has published on a wide variety of topics. His book *Porno? Chic!* explores the research on pornography and the sexualization of culture, arguing that pornography has helped societies to advance in female empowerment and acceptance of sexual minorities.

Heather McPherson—Heather is a sex therapist in Austin, Texas, writing about the role of technology and sexuality on modern relationships. She is the creator of the Southwest Sexual Health Alliance, a group dedicated to providing sexuality information and training to mental health and medical clinicians, in order to correct the level of sexual ignorance that plagues these fields.

Neil Malamuth, Ph.D.—Neil is simply the world's leading expert on the effects of porn on sexual violence. He is one of the few writers in this area who has done ACTUAL empirical research involving porn exposure. He maintains a balanced, thoughtful perspective about porn, a perspective based on what the data show, as opposed to what his opinions or beliefs are. He's a UCLA researcher with an extensive, decades-long list of objective, research-based publications.

John Mercer—John is a British academic in media studies, co-founder of the journal *Porn Studies*, and the author of *Gay Pornography: Representations of Sexuality and Masculinity*. His work helps to correct the way that porn discussions ignore the existence of gay porn, and how gay porn challenges blanket assumptions of misogyny and sexism.

Charles Moser, MD—Charles is San Francisco-based physician who works extensively with sexual minority groups. He has also published numerous articles examining the ethical, scientific, and diagnostic issues that are often ignored in the rush to pathologize sexual diversity.

Jim Pfaus, Ph.D.—Jim's research on sexual neurochemistry, learning and how these processes relate to sexual behaviors represents some of the best current understanding of modern brain science. Plus, he's got a great sense of humor. Anyone who can publish the terms "jacket-on" "jacket-off" (sound it out) in scientific literature is a-ok in my book.

Nicole Prause, Ph.D.—Nicole is a psychologist and researcher in California. She's an innovative, driven and passionate scientist who believes in confronting poor science and shaming in sexuality. Her work on the neurobiology of sexual behaviors, neuro-electrical stimulation, and sexual arousal is moving the field forward in fascinating ways. Prause has published several articles debunking the poor science and theory in sex and porn addiction.

Barry Reay, Ph.D.—Barry is a New Zealand professor of history, who undertook to examine and document the history of the Sex Addiction movement and industry. His work *Sex Addiction: A Critical History* reveals much of the history of sex addiction that has gone unnoticed, particularly the long trend of anti-homosexuality that has pervaded this conservative cultural movement.

Rory Reid, Ph.D.—Rory is a UCLA researcher and clinician

with a long history of researching pornography and sex addiction. He was the lead researcher on the DSM-5 trials for the proposed hypersexual disorder. Rory is committed to understanding what the data say about sexuality, pornography and hypersexual behaviors. Though we sometimes disagree, our disagreements are always based on the data as opposed to conviction or belief.

Adam Safron, Ph.D.—Adam is a professor at Northwestern and is a brilliant brain and neurochemistry researcher. He has an exceptional history of research and publication regarding sexual arousal and bisexuality in males along with issues related to mindfulness and depression.

Michael Seto, Ph.D.—Michael is a forensic psychologist in Canada, who has done extraordinary work on pedophilia and child pornography. His work has used research and data, rather than fear to move forward the dialogue about online sexual offending.

Krystelle Shaugnessy, Ph.D.—Australian researcher studying online sexual activities, sexual attitudes, and cybersex, with forthcoming publications and research on international outcomes of porn use.

Clarissa Smith, Ph.D.—British professor of sexual cultures, Clarissa is co-editor of the new academic journal *Porn Studies*, which publishes academic and research articles about pornography with an intent to examine porn in a larger context beyond the "porn causes rape" debate. Her presentation in the Intelligence Squared debate on "Pornography is Good For Us" is a stellar representation of the best understanding of porn.

Richard Sprott—Richard is a California psychologist, and head of the Community-Academic Consortium for Research on

Alternative Sexualities (CARAS). CARAS hosts an annual confer-
ence on alternative sexualities. With New York therapist David Ortmann, Richard published the book *Sexual Outsiders,* exploring the
world of BDSM through a non-pathologizing lens.

Alexander Stulhofer, Ph.D.—Stulhofer is a European sociologist
and researcher in Zagreb, Croatia, and head of the department of
sexology. He is the leader in sex therapy in Croatia, and his research
in recent years has involved examining porn use and sex in those
often called sex or porn addicts. His work demonstrates the danger
of the addiction model and how these labels have infiltrated outside
the United States.

Rebecca Sullivan, Ph.D. and Alan McKee, Ph.D. together published
one of the most dense, thorough and objective reviews of research,
policy and debate on pornography, *Pornography: Structures, Agency and
Performance (Key Concepts in Media and Cultural Studies).* Their work
makes the strong argument that much of the debate on porn has happened without the voices of porn performers, regarding their work
and the media. I once recommended they be awarded the "Indiana
Jones Award" for bravest academics, for their fearless and tireless efforts wading into a morass of conflicting research about pornography.

Kim Wallen, Ph.D.—Emory University professor Kim Wallen studies sex differences, sexual hormones, and research with primates
and neuroanatomy. He is also an expert on petroglyphs, and his
photographs inspired several of the petro-porn drawings depicted
in this book.

Lawrence Walters, Esq.—Lawrence is the preeminent First Amend-
ment scholar and attorney in the US, when it comes to porn. He's
been involved in the highest-profile cases involving attempts to

declare porn obscene and has defended both porn makers and porn consumers.

Mary Ann Watson, Ph.D.—Mary Ann is a psychologist and professor in Denver, with an extensive history of publications examining sexuality throughout the world, issues of gay parenting and cultural differences in sexuality. Her 2011 article exploring the positive effects and educational uses of pornography challenges the assumptions that pornography is inherently negative and detrimental.

Paul Wright Ph.D. - Paul is an Indiana University media professor who has studied pornography and masculinity extensively. His research includes some of the only longitudinal research examining the relationships between pornography and mental health/coping in men, demonstrating that in most cases, negative emotions such as loneliness precede increases in pornography use.

Ethical Porn Resources

Here are some websites and porn companies who are committed to making ethical porn. But more importantly, here are some of the people who are leading the charge toward making and distributing porn. These are the people who are the real resources. Websites and companies might come and go. But these people are trying to make porn better and make it more ethical for you the consumer, and for the performer. If you want to support ethical porn, follow these folks and support what they do. This isn't an exhaustive list by any means, and I hope that it is quickly outstripped by the growth of new producers and performers of ethical porn.

Buck Angel—Buck is a transman and a leading voice in trans porn and sex worker rights. Buck is smart, ethical, thoughtful, and committed to supporting performers. His films present trans performers as people with histories, depth and needs. If trans porn is your thing, start with Buck.

Jerry Barnett—Jerry runs a group in the UK called "Sex and Censorship." It's on Twitter @pornpanic. Jerry is a champion against censorship and demonizing of porn by the conservative government there. He's a leading expert on the legal issues regarding porn in the UK. He has a new book coming out about these issues.

Violet Blue—Violet is an expert on all things technical and Internet, especially when it involves sexuality. Her website/newsletter Tiny Nibbles has been promoting the ideas of ethical porn long before anyone else really knew what that meant. Violet's books on porn for women and Internet privacy are must-have resources.

jessica drake—jessica has been one of the most successful adult performers in recent years. Her educational series "jessica drake's Guide to Wicked Sex" has been honored by women, and drake's efforts to include and empower women are evident in her educational films. She is now combining her experience with her passion for sexual education.

Ethical Porn Partnership—a group started by Nichi Hodgson, which has as its mission to support and advocate for responsibly made porn. The group includes performers, producers, and consumers of porn as well as a listing of the values they endorse in ethical porn. http://ethicalporn.org

The Feminist Porn Awards—not a person, but a celebration of those performers and producers who are creating sexy, powerful pornography in a way that empowers all people involved and celebrates women's sexuality and autonomy.

Cindy Gallop—Cindy runs the website Makelovenotporn.com, a labor of love by her. Cindy is a champion for making ethical porn that shows real sex, and encourages a dialogue about the differences between real sex and porn sex, without abandoning the value of either form. Performers who submit porn to her website get 50 percent of the revenues, a testament to Cindy's commitment.

Nate Glass—Nate runs Takedown Piracy, a service that protects the copyright of adult material online. Nate and his team are some of the warriors who are out there fighting to keep porn legal and to ensure that the people who make and star in porn don't get robbed.

Conner Habib—Conner is a former English teacher turned porn star/writer/lecturer. His article "What I Want to Know Is Why You Hate Porn Stars?" from Seattle's *The Stranger* is one of the most eye-opening pieces you will read about how porn stars feel as they watch society tear them apart and shame them for their work.

Tina Horn—Tina is a writer and podcaster committed to exploring the worlds of sex work, kink, and sex education for everyone. Her book on *Sexting for Grownups* is a non-shaming exploration of how adults can use technology in fun, sexy ways. Her podcast "Why Are People Into That?" is a blast and recommended listening for all sex geeks.

Shine Louise Houston—Pink and White is the brainchild of Shine Louise Houston, a filmmaker honored with multiple Feminist Porn Awards. Shine, and Pink and White is a leader in ethical porn production, supporting consent, safe sex options, drug-free filming, and even trigger warnings in some of their material. Her film series "Crash Pad" is a queer, trans friendly, feminist collection.

Devon Hunter—briefly made gay porn with Anteros Media, producing material that focused on performers who were "out" gay men, in a style that celebrated genuine connection, consent, kindness and sensuality. http://www.devonhunter.info

Kink.com—one of the largest BDSM sites. With a diversity of genders, orientations and fetish material, Kink.com has also been one of the industry leaders in honoring consent in BDSM and in safe sex.

Jiz Lee—Jiz is a gender-queer performer who has become one of the most vocal advocates for ethical porn. Jiz is a dear friend and a brilliant person. Jiz' book *Coming Out Like a Porn Star* is required reading if you want to understand porn performers as people, who deserve ethical, responsible pay, and treatment.

Lorelei Lee—Lorelei is a famous fetish porn star, who has a history of performing and producing bondage and fetish videos with a variety of sites and companies. She's been involved in some of the cases in recent years, regarding legal challenges toward fetish films. She's an advocate against requirements for condoms in porn and has written eloquently against the demeaning and dismissive ways that general news media presents porn performers.

Eric Paul Leue—Eric works for the Free Speech Coalition. Eric was Mr. Leather Los Angeles and has become a leading advocate for performers, and for use of PrEP as way of preventing HIV transmission during sex and sex on film.

Louise Lush—Louise also known as Ms. Naughty, runs the website BrightDesire.com in Australia. Her films focus on feminism, porn for women, and even reclaiming the "vanilla" porn genre of heterosexuality without repeating all the clichés of past porn. Distinct from many filmmakers in porn, she celebrates the "ordinary" sex that most people are having and wants to find a way to make hot porn about it. Louise is also the inventor of the brilliant term "Panicdotal Evidence" to describe the ways that anti-porn campaigns are often built on exaggerated, inflated evidence based on unsubstantiated anecdotes.

Erika Lust—Erika is a European porn producer, who is staunchly feminist and wants to produce works that encourage women to enjoy and celebrate porn. She runs Erikalust.com and is committed to changing porn for the better, promoting the hashtag: #ChangePorn.

Maggie McNeill—Maggie runs the blog The Honest Courtesan and is a champion for sex worker rights. She is one of the leading voices opposing the current panic over sex-trafficking and the use of sex-trafficking claims to shut down legitimate sex workers.

Brooke Magnanti—Brooke is better known as Belle du Jour, from her days working as an escort in London while she was completing her Ph.D. in forensic pathology. Brooke writes about being a sex worker and has done a tremendous amount to destigmatize sex work. She's been a leading voice in the United Kingdom over the censorship and filtering efforts of recent years.

Kelsey Obsession—Kelsey runs a website focusing on specialty types of porn, from "giantess" porn to farting porn. Kelsey has a Ph.D. and is one of the smartest, most thoughtful folks in porn that

I've met. She works hard to make sure that the performers on her site are well-treated and well-paid.

Chanel Preston—Chanel is a porn performer, speaker and current President of the Adult Performer Advocacy Committee (APAC). APAC, Preston and Ela Darling, APAC Secretary, work to advocate for safe, healthy and consensual conditions for adult performers, both on and off the set.

Dan Savage—Dan really needs no introduction to most people who've been reading about sex or porn. But, many people continue to discover him anew and discover their own sexuality through reading his advice column, books, listening to his podcast or watching the YouTube video series "It Gets Better." But for all his influence, Dan remains one of the kindest men I've ever met. He's open about his sexuality and life, and he is a role model for us all. His homegrown erotic film festival, Hump, is developed and produced with ethical intentionality in a way that celebrates sex, consent, and community.

Dee Severe—with her husband, Dee runs Severe Sex, a fetish film producer specializing in femdom, BDSM material. Dee has distributed to the porn industry a video produced by her company, which educates viewers about consent, safe words, boundaries and limits within BDSM activity.

Tristan Taormino—Tristan has been the pioneer of feminist pornography, has a fabulous and popular podcast Talk Out Loud, and has written extensively about porn and sexuality. She is committed to making ethical porn and is a never-ending champion for performers' rights.

Courtney Trouble—Courtney runs the film company TROUBLE-films, which produces porn including a diversity of orientations, genders and body types, focusing on queer porn.

ABOUT THE AUTHOR

Dr. David J. Ley is an internationally recognized expert on issues related to sexuality, pornography and mental health. He has appeared on television with Anderson Cooper, Katie Couric, Dr. Phil and others. He has been interviewed in publications ranging from the *LA Times* and the *London Telegraph* to *Playboy* and *HUSTLER* magazines. Dr. Ley has published extensively in both the academic and "pop" realms of literature. His two books, *The Myth of Sex Addiction* (2012) and *Insatiable Wives* (2009) were revolutionary explorations of sexual issues, which blended a powerful client-centered narrative with a rich understanding of psychology, biology, and sociology. At the same time, he is Executive Director of a large behavioral health and substance abuse outpatient program and consults across the country on both mental health and sexuality-related issues. He has years of work with people as a practicing psychologist addressing sexuality issues. As a result, Dr. Ley is able to bring a broad, practical approach to help people effectively address sexuality-related issues. He is on Twitter, @DrDavidLey.